Love
Two lives, one …

'A spiritual classic',
Giles Mercer

'Totally absorbing. Haunting',
Ann Orr-Ewing

Other books by John Symons

also published by Shepheard-Walwyn

A Tear in the Curtain, 2013

"The history of Russia, but in a form that you will not have read it before ... objective and intensely personal. It tells us more in a few pages than many more formal accounts manage in a whole volume."
MICHAEL BOURDEAUX
Founder of the Keston Institute, Oxford

The Devil's Dance, 2014

Love is His Meaning

Two lives, one marriage

John Symons

SHEPHEARD-WALWYN (PUBLISHERS) LTD

© John Symons 2019

The right of John Symons to be identified as the author of this work has been asserted by him in accordance with the Copyright, Designs and Patents Act, 1988.

All rights reserved. No part of this book may be reproduced in any form without the written permission of the publisher, Shepheard-Walwyn (Publishers) Ltd

First published in 2018 by
Shepheard-Walwyn (Publishers) Ltd
107 Parkway House, Sheen Lane,
London SW14 8LS
www.shepheard-walwyn.co.uk

British Library Cataloguing in Publication Data
A catalogue record of this book
is available from the British Library

ISBN: 978-0-85683-528-5

Typeset by Alacrity, Chesterfield, Sandford, Somerset
Printed and bound in the United Kingdom
by 4edge Limited

Contents

	Preface	xi
1	Dad, 1953	1
2	Florence Louisa and William	6
3	'On Chorea'	11
4	'One and All'	17
5	India	23
6	'Floruit'	32
7	Commissioned	41
8	Matchmaking	46
9	Home Leave	54
10	Interlude	61
11	Dear Octopus	63
12	'When you and I were seventeen'	81
13	'Tea at Gunters'	87
14	'The test of the heart is trouble'	97
15	Interlude	108
16	Courtship and Marriage	110
17	Home Thoughts from Abroad	114
18	Making a Home	128
19	'Huntington's explains it all'	138
20	Number 10	146

21	At Risk	155
22	The Two of Them, Together	167
23	Interlude	176
24	No Way Out	178
25	'I love you, my darling'	184
26	'... down to Oxford's towers'	193
27	'Dearly loved husband, father and brother'	195
28	A New Life	202
29	Windwhistle	211
30	Neighbours and Friends	215
31	A Pattern of Life	222
32	Time Passes	228
33	'Gone are the days...'	238
34	'What can't be cured...'	247
35	'The best thing that ever happened to me...'	251
36	'A Ring of Faithfulness'	254
37	A Last Gift	262
38	'Such sweet sorrow'	265
39	A Walk	268
	Epilogue	271
	Acknowledgements	273

My parents' story is told from memory, documents and interviews with those who knew them well. It is all true.

*Judy, my wife,
never met Dad but
knew and loved Mum:
my three guides and companions
on The Way.*

*For Alan and Mavora Forward,
our faithful friends.*

Preface

EVERYONE KNOWS that, in our country and in many others, most people rarely go to church, but express a deep interest in spirituality. They are at home with a belief in a supreme spirit and perhaps feel a spiritual presence in their lives, but not with a faith connected with organizations and meeting together in buildings week by week.

In this book I would like to ask any reader a question, and I will explain how I came to face it for myself. It arose from rewriting, as one book, *Stranger on the Shore* and *This Life of Grace*, in the form that the story demands. This has allowed me to draw together into one volume the separate stories of my parents, and of their families, before they were married, and the story of their marriage and of my Mum's life after Dad's death, a widowhood of twenty-five years.

This treatment, of parallel lives, gives something of a picture of life in our country over the whole of the twentieth century. Perhaps there are worse ways to grasp what life was like for many ordinary families and working people in those years. It was a time when many more people went to church quite often, about fifty per cent of the population, as big a proportion in 1958 as had attended in 1914.

The questions that I dare to address to any reader are these: do you think that the current interest in spirituality would have enabled my parents to face what they faced together, in the way they did? If not, what is added by the faith which they professed, and is that faith true?

Perhaps the words of Mother Julian of Norwich point us to the answer:

> Do you want to know what our
> Lord meant in all this?
> Know it well.
> Love was his meaning.
> Who showed it to you?
> Love.
> Why did He show it to you?
> For Love.
> Remain firm in this love, and you will taste of it
> ever more deeply...
> In this love He has made all things for our benefit,
> and in this love our life is everlasting...
> In this love we have our beginning,
> and all this we shall see in God without end.

Julian of Norwich, *Revelations of Divine Love*, chapter 86.

1
Dad, 1953

THE WOODEN SCRUBBING BRUSH, with its sharp, spiky bristles, moves to and fro on the kitchen table. A little crescent wave of shallow water flows in front of it. And gripping the brush firmly and wielding it vigorously were Dad's hands. There is a rubbing, grating sound, so intense is his effort.

You might catch a glimpse of a pale blue and red tattoo on Dad's inner arm, in the gap above the button of his shirtsleeve. Dad nearly always wore his sleeves rolled down. The table was of pine, before pine became fashionable; before fashion existed where we lived. Dad used to scrub it every week. He bent low over it – for he was a little over six feet tall – working with a block of hard green or yellow soap in his left hand, and all his elbow grease.

The table stood in the kitchen by the window, opposite the Rayburn that was Dad's pride and joy. My younger brother and I used to play under it, imagining that it was a spaceship. We made a little control panel from a block of wood to which we nailed a few revolving wheels from one of the carriages of our clockwork train set. We sat there, partly hidden by the tablecloth, sometimes with our dog Patch, as we cruised around the

Universe, or at least our solar system, in this makeshift cabin. We were good brothers, two and a half years between us. We took it in turns to play the Captain, called Toby.

With a tie around his waist in place of a belt to make fast his corduroy trousers, fawn and well-worn, and wearing a shirt without its collar, Dad came to grips with the stains made by our pencils or crayons, or the splashes from our plates.

It was Dad who inspired our game. One week in three Dad worked a nightshift, and he loved to observe the positions of the stars and planets as they changed through the seasons. He read a good deal about astronomy. He used to talk to me about space and time, creation, and the wonders of life and the Universe.

Dad was always ashamed of the tattoos on his arms and chest. It was a 'silly thing', he thought, done by him in his earliest Army days. After he came back to England from India in 1947, after twenty-five years there, Dad never swam. Mum told us (and we believed her) that that was because the sea was too cold for him here, and perhaps it was, but now I can understand that it was also because of that sad sense of shame.

It was sad partly because Dad's first words were remembered in his family as, 'I could SWUM!' He was only three years old at the time that he said this to his mother and father, who like their forebears for generations, probably centuries, worked a precarious living from the waters around West Cornwall. His mother had told him not to go into the water until he could swim, a typical piece of Cornish drollery. In his youth Dad became such a powerful swimmer that he could swim to St Michael's Mount and back from Newlyn Harbour, about six miles, and in the Army he was a superb athlete. But in my childhood, on holiday at the seaside, Dad held our towels on the shore and waited at the water's edge while we swam.

In fact, I loved the pale colours and the fading shapes of the tattoos. Dad was happy to let them be seen briefly sometimes in the summer when, with his sleeves rolled up, he swept the garden paths.

As his hands wield the scrubbing brush, easing out all the grease and dirt of the past week, sometimes both hands together, sometimes just the right, you can see that they are browned by the sun of all his years in India: strong and hard hands, yet also gentle and sensitive. They have undertaken all manner of work of the heaviest sort in Cornwall, in Ireland and in the East. They have gripped a pewter beer tankard as he sat outside his tent in the heat of the jungle. But they have also carefully turned the pages of the Book of Common Prayer and the Bible at worship in St Peter's Church at Saugor, in the Central Provinces of India, and they have received the elements of the Holy Communion. They held his mother in an embrace during the last hours of her life and comforted her. They received his first son with delight from Mum when she presented me to him outside his bungalow in India in February 1946. I can see the joy and humour in his face in the photographs of that event. He had waited forty-four years for children of his own. You can see the same character in his face that you sense in his hands.

There is only one photograph of Dad with his mother and his six sisters. All seven children are gathered around Florence Louisa, perhaps on the day of her husband William's funeral in November 1914. There is

no photograph of all eight of the family together with William, who had been a fisherman and a member of the Royal Naval Volunteer Reserve. His death followed some early action at sea in the First World War. But there, at the focal point of this single photograph of his family, rests Dad's right hand – gently, firmly – on Florence Louisa's left shoulder, comforting and reassuring her. He was not yet thirteen years old.

And there it is again, resting lightly on my right shoulder in another photograph taken when I was six years old. The four of us are standing in front of a line of trees. We had been gathering mushrooms. Dad's left hand, cupped to hold some of them, is on my left shoulder, and his trilby hat is partly visible, lying on the lush

grass to our right. Beyond the trees, in the valley of the River Plym, our village of Plympton is already rapidly expanding. Within twenty years it will be little more than a dormitory suburb of Plymouth.

But in the photograph there is a contrast with the steadiness of Dad's touch on my shoulders. It is the look on his face. What does it show? Worry? Uncertainty? Confusion? Perhaps I also look confused or quizzical. What is happening? Time will tell.

2
Florence Louisa and William

DAD WAS BORN in December 1901. He was the only son and the eldest child in the family. My Auntie Florrie, named after their mother, and the first of six sisters, was born a couple of years later. It was she who helped me to build up a picture of their life. I had been too young to take it all in properly when Dad was alive and well.

Auntie Florrie lived longer than the others and she was in good health almost to the end of her ninety-one years. In the 1980s and 1990s, as her life began to draw to a close, I used to travel down from London and visit her at Heamoor, only a hundred yards from Wesley Rock Chapel, where her parents were married. She lived in Wesley Street quietly with her youngest son, Coulson, in the well-built stone cottage that had come to her through her late husband, Charlie Paul.

The sleeper from Paddington used to arrive at Penzance, at the end of the line, by about 8 o'clock. I would take a taxi and call in at a florist's shop to buy Auntie Florrie some freesias or anemones, and then, at number 3 Wesley Street, she would give me a Cornish welcome and a grand breakfast of eggs and bacon and fried bread. Wearing a long apron over her cardigan and tweed skirt, she wielded her frying pan and fish-slice boisterously. She stood straight for her years. Her thick grey hair, her quiet smile, the shape and angle of her forehead and her dark, blue-grey eyes spoke to me of Dad, and I dare to believe that, in some way, I made his presence real for her.

Then we got down to business. Sitting at the kitchen table by the fireplace with paper and pencil, we would roam over what she remembered of her family's life. Coulson would stay on the edge of this, listening with interest to parts of the conversation, never making his presence and keen attention too obvious to his mother, moving in and out of the kitchen, sometimes going for a while into the back yard where red pelargoniums and other bright flowers grew strongly in carefully tended pots.

Coulson told me that, whenever he asked Auntie Florrie about the family, she used to say, 'Why do you want to know about that? You never know what you might find out if you ask questions like that!' But with me she was always at ease and open in talking about the family. She seemed to delight in passing on what she alone now knew. Often she seemed to sense in advance the questions I was about to ask, particularly when the matter was sad, and then we would shed a few quiet tears together, but just as often we laughed at stories from the past. Perhaps we both knew that time was short; the years were running out. We were talking just in the nick of time.

At the end of the morning I would gather all my papers into my briefcase and Auntie Florrie would take out of the oven three of her golden-brown Cornish pasties. Coulson would join us. And then I would be away, usually for another twelve months, on the train heading for London.

I owe Auntie Florrie so much.

Like Auntie Florrie, Dad loved and revered their mother, Florence Louisa and their father, William.

William and his father John Hocking Symons, and their ancestors, had lived in the far west of Cornwall and worked the seas around Newlyn, or laboured on the land there, for all of the nineteenth century, and probably for many centuries before that. It is a surprise that, by contrast, John Hocking's wife Peace and her family came from the industrial towns of Batley and Dewsbury, just south of Bradford and Leeds in Yorkshire.

Probably, in the mid-1860s, John Hocking visited the east coast and for a while worked on the fishing fleet at Scarborough – that is what his grandchildren believed – when the fishing was bad in the western seas off Newlyn. He moved inland to Mirfield and married, but his first wife died only two years later of tuberculosis, 'phthisis' in the medical language of those days. They had no children.

John Hocking stayed on in the Mirfield area, working at an iron foundry, and in due course he met Peace there. They married in 1875. In 1881 the Census records that the family was living in Jack Lane in Newlyn.

At the time of the Census in April 1901 John Hocking was still working as a fisherman, but he was no longer fit. His three eldest sons, Frank, William and Ernest, all in their early twenties, were fishermen, and perhaps they joked with him that he had been at sea too long – even on land he seemed to keep his sea legs and to sway unsteadily. That was not because of drink. The Wesleyan, teetotal influence was strong in Newlyn. John Hocking and Peace and their family were Methodists. Perhaps the young men thought that the same thing would happen to them if they stayed at sea for too long. Had not their grandfather, Frank, ended up like that, working as a labourer on the land at the end of his life, after so many years at sea, until he died of malaria? So, like his father before him, John Hocking sorted out and cleaned the nets on the quayside and left the fishing to his three eldest boys. The youngest son, and last child, Alfred, was only twelve years old, in his last year at school.

By the turn of 1901, when Queen Victoria died and, in the last moments of her life, sensed the presence of her consort Prince Albert and called out to him on her way to be reunited with him after so many years of widowhood, William had met Florence Louisa. Later that year they married.

Florence Louisa's background was much less settled than William's. The marriage certificate in August 1901 gives her full name as Florence Louisa Groves. She was twenty years old. No father is mentioned in her line in the certificate, which just reads: 'Florence Louisa Groves. 20 years. Spinster. Residence at time of marriage – Marine Place, Penzance.' No 'rank or profession' is listed.

The 1901 Census shows that in April that year Florence Louisa was living alone at 26 Back Marine Terrace. It states that she was nineteen years old and was working as a charwoman, but, seeing the family photograph taken in November 1914, someone said to me, 'You can see that she was a lady.' I can. Like Dad,

I too have come to love Florence Louisa for what she did and suffered; for what she was – for her loyalty and courage. Perhaps you will see what I mean.

Florence Louisa and William both signed the register after their wedding service, but John Hocking Symons, William's father, one of the witnesses of their marriage, made his mark with a cross. His hand was now too unsteady to write. Twenty-six years earlier he had been able to write his signature on his own marriage certificate, whereas Peace had made her mark with a cross.

So, on 4th August 1901 my grandparents were married in the chapel at Heamoor. The chapel had been built on the site of the Rock on which Wesley used to stand and preach the gospel in the fields a hundred and fifty years earlier. Wesley's work in the area led to many people being converted to a deep Christian faith, and they in their turn exerted a dramatic and beneficial influence on the morals and way of life in Penzance and Newlyn, and generally in west Cornwall for many years to come.

After the wedding William and Florence Louisa went to live at number 3 Marine Place. On 11th December Dad was born there.

The family lived for a little longer in Penzance, but soon William and Florence Louisa moved to Newlyn where they spent the rest of their short lives, living first at Paul Hill, then Duke Street, and then Paul Hill again.

Finally, in 1913 they settled at number 4 Jack Lane.

Dad's six sisters were born between his arrival at the end of 1901 and the outbreak of the Great War in August 1914: Florrie in 1903, Suzie in 1905, Nora in 1908, Rene in 1910, Clara in 1911, and Kathleen in 1913.

The family was complete.

3
'On Chorea'

IN 1907 DAD'S GRANDFATHER, John Hocking, died. On the death certificate the doctor stated that the cause of death was 'chorea exhaustion' as well as heart failure. There was more to his unsteadiness than his sons' jokes about sea legs on land had acknowledged.

What was his widow, Peace, to make of that obscure term? Perhaps she had heard of St Vitus' Dance. With its static population and the risk of inbreeding, west Cornwall, like other remote areas, was prey to hereditary illnesses.

And what did Dr Hart know about her husband's condition? How could a physician in west Cornwall in 1907 have read the 1872 issue of the *Medical and Social Reporter* of Philadelphia, in the United States, in which George Huntington published the scientific paper entitled 'On Chorea' that would for ever associate his name with this disease?

After all, John Hocking had lived to sixty-six years, a good age by the standards of the time and place and occupation. Two of his sons would die much younger. The day-to-day struggle to make a living was enough to exhaust all the energies of his sons and their families.

John Hocking was lucky, in a way, to have reached sixty-six years.

It all began with Chromosome 4.

It always begins with Chromosome 4, gene IT15, a few specks of matter.

Sometimes, perhaps in sixty cases in a million, a fault is there. No one knows why. It just happens. The coding of the gene is extended a little, and that unnecessary extension is the cause of it all.

If the fault is there in the gene, then it leads to Huntington's chorea, Huntington's disease, usually in middle age.

It is what they used to call St Vitus' Dance. Chorea means dance.

If a person has the Huntington's gene, each sperm or egg contains two copies of Chromosome 4, gene IT15, one inherited from each parent; one normal and one faulty.

So, if such a person marries a person without Huntington's, and they then have a child, the child inherits a normal Chromosome 4, gene IT15 from the healthy parent but either a normal or a faulty gene from the parent with Huntington's.

In this way, a child of someone with the disease has a 50-50 chance of inheriting it. It is as simple as that: a 50-50 chance, the toss of a coin. It never skips a generation.

Either way, the child's fate is sealed.

Inherit the faulty gene, and you develop Huntington's. Or inherit the healthy gene, and you see your afflicted parent disappear, fragment before your eyes, and die of the disease; and then, unless you take a genetic test to see if the coin landed heads or tails in your own case, you live with that question unresolved for the rest of your life.

This is the story of how this disease affected Dad and his six sisters, the lives of everyone in his family. It is the story of how they responded. Huntington's is a disease of families as well as those who die of it.

What impact the sight of his grandfather's illness and death had on Dad, I cannot tell. He was in only his sixth year when John Hocking died, and by then Peace was probably protecting, or screening, John Hocking from everyone, even from his young grandchildren. Dad told his younger sisters of his love for his grandmother and of her care for him as a little boy. He recalled how, each June, she used to hang elderflower blossoms from a beam in the kitchen 'to keep away the flies', but he never mentioned his grandfather. Perhaps he could not remember him at all. The only thing that Auntie Florrie could remember was that she had heard from someone that their grandfather was 'shaky' at the end of his life.

So John Hocking probably faded gradually from his grandchildren's life, leaving at most a hazy image in Dad's memory of an ailing grandfather, who died just after he had started to attend Wesley School in The Fradgan, in Newlyn.

In the years in which Dad and his sisters were born, William, their father was earning his living in several ways. His main occupation was with the fishing fleet in

Newlyn Bay, but his wages from that work were tiny and unpredictable. He also did general labouring and worked on the local farms. In addition, he joined the Royal Naval Reserve, and in 1910 and 1913 served in the Merchant Marine.

From her early years Florence Louisa suffered from poor health. She was often ill, especially after an operation of some sort on her neck. 'Our mother was never well,' Auntie Florrie told me. She made it a habit to eat as little as she could in order to have enough to feed the children. When she made Cornish pasties, she used to put all the meat in those that she cooked for her family, while in her own she would put just a scrap of bone to make a little juice to give flavour to the potato and swede. It was a 'bone pasty', Auntie Florrie said, after eighty years still in awe of her mother's loving kindness.

From his early years, as a schoolboy, Dad sometimes worked at the baker's shop at the top of Jack Lane (its successor, Eddy's Bakery, was there, selling pasties and bread and Cornish saffron cake, until 2007), and at other times he delivered newspapers.

About thirty yards along Jack Lane from where William, Florence Louisa and their growing family were living, William's brother Frank occupied another tiny cottage. Frank was two years older than William and, like him, was a fisherman. Frank never married. By and large, the men in the Symons family married in their thirties, and by that age Frank was already ill.

In the summer of 1910, when King Edward VII died and was succeeded by King George V, Dad was eight years old, and three of his sisters had been born. Already the first signs of their Uncle Frank's illness were visible, reminding the adults in the family of John Hocking's wasting illness and death, and slowly extending over the family the shadow of what was to befall Frank.

Then, only three months after the outbreak of war, William died. He had been serving as an Able Seaman on HMS Alexandra, and was involved in an early action against the Imperial German fleet. As a result of the engagement, many of the crew found themselves in the sea for some time. William's heart came under severe stress, and finally, after four days in the Royal Naval Hospital at Stonehouse in Devonport, gave way to acute pericarditis and the collapse of the mitral valve.

William was thirty six years old. He died before the Huntington's gene, which unwittingly he had passed on to his son and two of his daughters, could begin to do its work in him.

At the end of 1914 Frank moved house. The records are not clear. He may have settled with Florence Louisa and her children after William's death, but more probably he joined his mother, Peace, who was by then living with his brother Alfred and his wife Maud and their two daughters, in yet another cottage in Jack Lane.

The other remaining Symons brother, Ernest, probably also lived nearby. He and his wife Ellen, in the course of time, produced a family of eight children.

Among William's generation, Maud, Alfred's wife, lived longest. She was still alive when I married in 1971. By then doctors knew more about Huntington's disease. I wanted to find out what I could about its effects on my family and the prospects for my future and that of my wife-to-be.

At my request, but reluctantly, Mum asked Florrie about it. I suggested that great-aunt Maud might know more than anyone else and be able to help.

The time was not right. Auntie Florrie was not yet able to speak openly about it all. She seemed to resent my questions. In her letter to Mum she wrote,

> Jack is a wonderful person and the boys need to be proud of him, as I'm sure Jack is proud of his family.

Auntie Florrie's wounds were still raw, too tender to touch. That is the way it often is for families with Huntington's disease. It is a disease of families, not just individuals, but its effects on families can sometimes be overcome.

Fifteen years later I began my visits to see Auntie Florrie at Heamoor and could try to unravel the truth with her. By then, the time was right.

Much later, after her death, cousin Coulson told me that the long, quiet talks I had with her in her last years had helped Auntie Florrie and him, as well as me, to come to terms with our family's past. The three of us were lucky to have those days together; they gave us joy. Dad would have been pleased. It was as if he was there with us, bringing us his gift of peace.

4
'One and All'

WILLIAM'S DEATH and Florence Louisa's poor health almost snuffed out Dad's family.

At first the local authorities wanted to separate the children, aged between one and thirteen years, and put them out to be fostered. Somehow, Florence Louisa managed to prevent this and to bring them up together.

Seventy-five years later, Auntie Florrie told me that it was the tanners that Dad earned that saved the family. Florence Louisa's devotion, Dad's 'tanners', the common sense of the six girls, and the shrewd, watchful eye of Peace somehow kept them together. As a war widow, Florence Louisa received a tiny pension from the Royal Navy.

Somehow they all survived. Jack, Florrie and Suzie, the three eldest children, successfully brought up the younger sisters. They shared the work among themselves. Jack earned what he could; Florrie and Suzie took care of their mother, Jack and their younger sisters.

Dad left school in 1915, soon after his thirteenth birthday. You can see his intelligence and longing to learn in the school photograph that Florence Louisa and his sisters gave him as a birthday present when he left school. Dad is standing, already tall, next to the young teacher. On the back is the only example of Florence Louisa's writing, in pencil: 'To our darling Jack from Mother and Sisters wishing you many happy returns of your birthday' (followed by 24 kisses.)

Dad went to work for Dick Bath, the coal merchant at Newlyn harbour, 'heaving coal', as Auntie Florrie put it. He later drove the firm's horse and cart to make coal deliveries. He stayed there for almost three years.

In 1916 Florrie went 'into service'. At first, she worked locally at Faugan farm, walking there and back every day from Jack Lane. She remembered the grandmother of the family at the farm making cream by hand and churning butter; the son of the family was away at the War in France.

When Suzie in turn left school in 1918 and was able to do more at home, Florrie could move to better paid work. She visited Peace's family, the Crawshaws, in Yorkshire, and they put her in touch with a doctor in

Hertfordshire for whose family she worked for a few months. But after that short absence from Cornwall, she returned home and went to live and work in the village of Pendeen. There she worked for the family of Captain Hitchens. Florrie managed to get home once a week, and, like Jack, shared her wages with the family. She remained in service at Pendeen until her marriage in 1926.

These years brought the three eldest children very close to one another, especially Jack and Suzie, who were living at home and caring for the family. As Florence Louisa's health worsened – she was suffering from tuberculosis – she started to spend much of her time, and to sleep by night, in a little wooden shed on the far side of the back yard of their cottage. Perhaps this helped her breathing, but she did it mainly to protect her children from the disease. At that time the cause of tuberculosis was unknown and there was no cure. She taught Suzie to cook. Because of her care, none of the children developed TB, and all of them, except Kathleen, the youngest, were fit. Kathleen suffered, from her early years, from rheumatic fever.

Life was a struggle. At the end of the Great War conditions had not eased in Great Britain. Prices continued to rise rapidly in 1919 and the early 1920s. There was an uneasy spirit of turmoil fermenting in the country. The government was hard pressed to maintain social peace and security. It introduced some political and social reforms, but the mood did not improve much.

In 1919 the Prime Minister, David Lloyd George, spoke some words in the House of Commons about the crisis that even caught the attention of Lenin and the Bolsheviks in Moscow, giving them hope in the middle of the Russian civil war when power seemed, for a while, to be slipping away from them. In a speech that was quoted in history textbooks in Russia, even after the end of Communism there in 1991, Lloyd George was reported to have said:

> All Europe is seething with the fever of revolution ... Everywhere there is not so much a spirit of dissatisfaction as of anger or vengeance among working men, even open fury against the conditions which they experienced before the War. The popular masses of Europe, from one end to the other, put in question the future of all the existing order, all the current political, social and economic structures of society.
>
> (My translation of a Russian textbook)

In 1920, Lloyd George's government wished to support Poland against Soviet Russia after the Red Army, on Lenin's orders, had marched on Warsaw and was defeated by the Poles. The British trade unions forced Lloyd George to back down and to withdraw the government's ultimatum to Russia. This experience so encouraged Lenin in his conviction that world revolution was on its way that he said:

> We have reached the English proletariat ... Political forces in England are at that stage of development that we Bolsheviks enjoyed in Russia after February 1917 when the Soviets were compelled to control each step of the bourgeois government ... It is a dyarchy.[1]

---

[1] The historical significance of this is a theme of my book about Russia, 'A Tear in the Curtain', published by Shepheard-Walwyn. Joint rule, or dyarchy, for Lenin denoted the period in 1917, after the democratic revolution of February until the Biolshevik seizure of power in October, when the 'soviets', or councils of workers, dominated by Lenin's supporters, manipulated the liberal Provisional Government to suit the Bolsheviks' purposes.

Although the political and economic crisis in Great Britain gradually eased, it remained a struggle for Florence Louisa's family, like so many others, to survive.

Dad sensed that he had to do something decisive for himself and his family. At first Florence Louisa was upset and worried when he told her what he had in mind. She had lost her husband to the Germans in the War and now, when Ireland and the Continent were still in chaos and some countries were suffering revolution and fresh bloodshed, her only son planned to join the Army.

But Dad, Florrie and Suzie had worked out together what needed to be done. The family needed more money and their mother more medicines and better food. Dad said, 'I won't spend the rest of my life heaving coal for Dick Bath for a few shillings a week.' Only the Army offered him clothing, regular food, a steady wage and enough to send something home. It was also a great attraction for him that it would give him more education.

In the end Florence Louisa accepted the good sense of what her three eldest children had decided. On St George's day, 23rd April 1919, Dad joined the British Army. He signed on as a private soldier with the Duke of Cornwall's Light Infantry (DCLI) at Bodmin. His Army service book lists his trade on joining up as 'horse-driver'. When I was a little boy Dad used to say to me, 'You can drive a horse to the trough, but you can't make him drink.' He was speakng from experience.

For the next three years Dad served with the second battalion of the DCLI in Ireland, at Ballyshannon in County Donegal and in County Clare in the war against the Irish Republican Army. It was a bitter war and a hard life. At that time he said, 'If anyone from Newlyn says that he wants to join the Army, take him to the harbour and throw him in.'

Early in 1921 Florence Louisa became critically ill. Dad was given compassionate leave to visit her in Cornwall. He arrived home on a Thursday and had a long talk with his mother. The next day, 17th February, Florence Louisa died peacefully in his arms.

In addition to her 'generalised tuberculosis', the doctor certified that the cause of death was 'inanition', wasting away or starvation caused by the poverty of their life, the effects of the long German blockade of Great Britain, and the economic turmoil arising from the Great War and its aftermath.

A month after Florence Louisa's death, Uncle Frank's life also came to its end. The cause of his death is recorded as 'chorea gravidum' and exhaustion. He was only forty four years old.

In December 1921 Ireland was partitioned. In the southern counties the Irish Free State was set up. After a terrible civil war there, comparative calm came to Ireland. Many regiments of the British Army, including Dad's, were withdrawn from the island, leaving a few in the six northern counties still loyal to the British Crown.

The only thing that Jack and his sisters could do was to soldier on in their different ways.

Together, Florence Louisa and William, against the odds, had created a family strong enough to stand the test of time.

5
India

THE END OF THE EMERGENCY in Ireland led to the withdrawal of Dad's regiment to England. The first battalion of the Duke of Cornwall's Light Infantry was to be sent to serve in India, where it would remain for many years, and Dad decided to transfer from the second battalion and go there with it.

Florence Louisa's tiny income from her widow's pension from the Royal Navy had died with her. By volunteering to go to India Dad would increase his pay a little, and would receive many other opportunities. He would be able to save and to send more money back home to help Florrie and Suzie to support their younger sisters.

This move gave Dad opportunities for travel and for learning a foreign language that, as a child, he could not have imagined would come to him. He came to love the Indians and India. He learnt so much about the world and its ways in the twenty-five years that he spent there.

His love of England and of India went hand in hand. He sometimes used to quote Kipling's line to me:

And what should they know of England who only England know?

On a Saturday morning in early December 1989 I am sitting at the kitchen table, after breakfast, with Auntie Florrie in Wesley Street. We have been working hard on the family tree and the story of the early days.

Auntie Florrie is still fit and well, so alert and interested, and so like Dad that I feel him there with us. She falls silent for a while at the end of our long talk. She stirs herself and suddenly flushes slightly – I have never before seen her colour change in this way – and then looks me straight in the eye, with Dad's calm grey eyes.

'They said that he was the best boy ever to leave Newlyn', she says. And then I know that it is true, as her sons and daughter told me, that Dad was, and remained, a hero for his sisters.

Dad found help and support at home when he was thinking about going to India. Florrie and Suzie encouraged him to go, although they all knew that it would be 1929 at the earliest before they would see one another again. A private soldier serving in India received home leave once every seven years.

Mr Phelps, the vicar of St Peter's church helped Dad to weigh everything up and to take the decision. Auntie Florrie remembered Dad going to talk to him about it.

The vicar knew the family well. After their father died, Florence Louisa's health grew worse and worse and she was house-bound. The seven children used to go on their own to Chapel and Church, turn and turn about, in the morning and evening. If they went to the Methodist chapel on Paul Hill in the morning, in the evening they would go to St Peter's church in The Coombe, built in the middle of Queen Victoria's reign.

Dad arrived in India in April 1922.

Over the next few years, five of his sisters married: Suzie in 1925, Florrie in 1926, Rene in 1929 and Clara and Nora in 1930. Dad, Clara and their youngest sister, Kathleen, were the three who developed Huntington's.

Just as a fragile stability was beginning to establish itself, Suzie died in childbirth in October 1925. It was a completely unnecessary death, Auntie Florrie told me. The death certificate records:

> Childbirth post partum haemorrhage and shock ... No P[ost] M[ortem].

Suzie's baby died, too.

By now Dad was well into his fourth year in India. Florrie wrote to give him the terrible news. Dad replied that he would arrange to come back to England and transfer to the second battalion of the DCLI serving there.

Florrie and the others wrote back to him immediately. They pressed him to stay on in India, and insisted that, together, they would cope. Not only was the pay better in India, which helped them all, but also Dad was beginning to flourish there. He was making a success of army life, and he was enjoying it much more than he had in England or Ireland.

As his sisters married and set up home and began to bring up their children, Dad's letters came to them with an amazing series of postmarks, which intrigued and lodged in the memories of his young nephews and nieces.

In those years the Duke of Cornwall's Light Infantry served at Chakrata in the hills between Derha Dun and Simla from 1922 to 1923; at Lucknow near Cawnpore (now Kanpur) from 1923 to 1927; and at Lebong in Darjeeling/Bengal from 1928 to 1930. From time to time Dad was able to travel a little. He laid down vivid memories of the Rivers Ganges and Jumna, and of Mt Kanchenjunga, the third highest mountain in the world, and above all of the patient nature of the Indian people, prepared to wait another week at the roadside if they missed this week's bus. He admired them for it. He always took the long, strategic view himself, and had the courage and loyalty to see things through to the end.

In the 1930s the regiment served from 1931 to 1934 at Bareilly, an important railhead and centre on the plain in the north of the United Provinces, not far from the border with Nepal. It moved to Razmak, on the North West frontier with Afghanistan in October 1934 and served there for a year until October 1935. The next postings for the regiment were to Dinapore, near Patna on the River Ganges from 1935 to 1937; and to Lahore in January 1938, in what is now Pakistan.

On a bookcase in my dining-room stand three silver cups. Dad bought a set of these bookcases for my brother and me when we were at primary school and were enthusiastically beginning to read.

The silver cups go back to the early years of Dad's time in India. One of them is dated '1927'. It commemorates the first prize won by Dad's tug-of-war team at the annual athletic sports of 19th Indian Infantry

Brigade, of which the first battalion of the DCLI formed a part.

There is a photograph, too, of the team which won the trophy in four successive years. The caption records 'Pte Symons' as a member of the

> 110 stone tug-of-war team.
> Winners of the Lucknow Brigade Cups and Medals 1924, 1925, 1926 and 1927.

In front of the ten men of the team, their coach (a company sergeant-major) and their commanding officer, Col. Goldsmith, is coiled the rope, perhaps two inches in diameter, and near it are displayed the winning team's cup and shield, and on either side of them, in two rows, the smaller cups presented to the team members.

But of course it is the image of Dad which holds my attention. How fit and well he looks, how completely at ease, how flourishing. Everything was going well for him in India, and for his remaining five sisters and their young families at Home. Dad is standing third from the left, behind Colonel Goldsmith.

None of Dad's many letters Home from those years survives, but one document does, much folded and a little worn. Dad kept it safe in his wallet for nearly fifty years, to the end of his life. The paper is marked in pencil, in Dad's own hand: '5430269 Pte W. Symons, A Coy, 1/DCLI Chakrata, India, 12/8/23'. It reads:

Personal Address to All Ranks by
Lt. Col. H.D. Goldsmith DSO
Commanding
1st Battalion, The Duke of Cornwall's Light Infantry.

On being gazetted to command the Battalion with which I have been connected for nearly 26 years, my chief feeling is one of pride at being at the head of a unit with such a long and distinguished record both in peace and war.

I wish to remind all ranks, however, that we must not be content to live on our past records, however glorious, and am confident that I can count on the loyal and whole-hearted cooperation of one and all to maintain and, if possible, to enhance the standard of soldierly excellence the Battalion has borne in the past.

We are shortly moving to a station, which is indelibly associated with our name. In and about Lucknow are the graves of some 400 Officers, NCOs, and men who gave their lives in the successful Defence of the Residency.[2]

---

[2] In the Indian Mutiny of 1857-8.

>   This success was due not to any one individual but to the stubborn courage, determination and devotion to duty of all ranks.
>
>   Wherever the Regiment has served, it has always earned a name for good sportsmanship, and good conduct, both in and out of barracks.
>
>   One of the best tributes ever paid to these traditions was in the farewell address to the Battalion in 1912 by the inhabitants of Gravesend, in which it was said that, by their conduct there, the Battalion had earned the name of a Regiment of Gentlemen.
>
>   I feel sure that every one of you will make it a point of honour to live up to that title, and to emulate the example set by our forefathers of the 32nd Foot in the past.
>
>   CHAKRATA 11.8.23   H.D. GOLDSMITH, LT-COLONEL

This strong sense of purpose and identity, of duty and principles, openly expressed, gave those who shared it a clear and honourable meaning for their lives. There truly was an ideal of a 'regiment of gentlemen' in the Battalion. There was a power in it. In Dad's case, this shared ideal was built on the Christian influence of his family and all that they had learnt together from his earliest years. These principles shaped his life. They helped him, and through him enabled his family, to find their way through what lay ahead.

※

In 1929 Dad became eligible for his first home leave. It was the year in which his sister Rene married Harold at St Peter's, Newlyn. Perhaps Dad was there and was able to give Rene in marriage at St Peter's, but there is no photograph of the wedding. No one now alive knows what happened when Dad came home in 1929 and how he and his sisters celebrated their time together.

Megan, Rene's daughter, told me, 'They were a close family; they didn't say much about the past.' As a result, most of the story of the inch-by-inch improvement in their lives is lost and with it the record of the events accompanying the family weddings and the births of the children of the new generation. One of Nora's sons, among the earliest of my cousins to be born, told me that he remembered his great-grandmother, Peace, showing him what everyone called 'Granny's box' at number 4 Jack Lane. In the box she kept the Family Bible, some photographs and the family's birth, marriage and death certificates. My cousin remembers seeing the box again in the years after Peace's death in 1931.

Not long after that, the box of family treasures was mislaid, probably when Nora and her family moved house away from the heart of Newlyn, near the harbour, where they had lived for so many years. The move was not of their choice. In the second half of the 1930s some of the houses in Jack Lane were designated for slum clearance. The labelling of the cottages as 'slums' provoked so much outrage among the locals that a small squadron of Newlyn's fishing vessels sailed up the English Channel to the River Thames and protested outside the Houses of Parliament. As a result, most of the cottages were reprieved, but number 4 was not saved.

Soon after the War, and ten years after Nora and the family moved out, number 4 Jack Lane was leveled to the ground. The plot that it had occupied became a car park.

'Granny's box' disappeared, and with it any photographs of Dad's home leave in 1929. So much of the story of those early years is now also lost.

6
'Floruit'

DAD RETURNED TO INDIA in the autumn of 1929. He settled into his second term of seven years there. Posted away from the first battalion of the Duke of Cornwall's Light Infantry, he was stationed at the Infantry Small Arms School at Pachmarhi in Central India. He served at the School for the rest of his career in the Army. The School was moved a hundred miles or so from there to the north, to Saugor, and expanded soon after the War broke out. Dad played an important role in organising that move. Many hundreds of officers and men, Indian and British, were to pass through the School on its six-week courses in the years of the War.

There were about 45,000 British troops in India in late 1929 when Dad began his posting at Pachmarhi. By that time he was an acting sergeant, and in 1932 he was promoted sergeant. On the 2nd of May 1935, 'by order of the Viceroy and Governor-General of India in Council', he was made a warrant-officer, and from that time until 1940 he was the Regimental Quarter-Master Sergeant at Pachmarhi.

Dad was keen to learn Urdu properly and to speak it well. In the April and October of 1933 he passed the lower and higher examinations in Urdu at Jubbalpore. He retained a strong and lively interest in languages for the rest of his life. The Army gave him the sixth-form education that he had missed as a boy. He passed his Higher National Certificate examinations, including English language and literature. He read widely. The signatures that he wrote in the books that he bought at that time show the beautiful copperplate hand that he had developed.

Perhaps these were Dad's happiest years. Pachmarhi is set in the Mahadeo hills, at 3,700 feet. There was a glorious climate to enjoy, comfortable for the British and the Indians. The little town and military cantonment were blessed with many tropical trees and beautiful vegetation, and surrounded by an exotic and mysterious landscape, with a river and waterfalls. Dad was doing work that he enjoyed. He had colleagues, British and Indian, whom he liked. The officers liked and respected him. By 1936 his commanding officer listed him as a man who deserved to be commissioned as a regular officer in the Indian Army. He loved the athletics and games, and enjoyed shooting. Above all, he was unbelievably fit.

※

Twenty-five years after Dad died, when Mum was lying in her hospital bed following a stroke, she said to me, 'How Dad did love you two boys!' She had been telling me that we had given him more happiness than anything else; she really believed it, and her mind was clear as she spoke. But by the time my brother and I were starting to attend school Dad was in his fifties and so much sadness was closing in on him, and indeed on all four of us. In the 1930s Dad had enjoyed steady progress and stability in his career, good friends and colleagues, and a healthy outdoor life at Pachmarhi, which Mum sometimes called his 'spiritual home', meaning his favourite place. He always regretted that he could not take her there.

When we were little boys, Dad used to tell us of his adventures from those days: marches and camps and hunts for man-eating tigers in the jungle; sleeping under the stars with his boots as a pillow and 'brushing' his teeth with a few grains of salt on his index finger; slaking his thirst in green pools of stagnant water; staying awake all night, camping on a small platform in the branches of a tree, with a goat's carcase tied to the trunk, waiting for the big game to arrive. On Saturday mornings when there was no school, we would perch on each side of Dad on the bed and he would tell us tales of those years.

The Romans and mediaeval scholars used to speak and write of the time of life at which a person 'flourished' – 'floruit'. They had in mind a conventional age, and they used the term to date their heroes and leaders in relation to each other. For many people, it seems, their 'floruit' is in the years between thirty-five and forty-five. However much they achieve later, whatever recognition they receive, it is in those years that they seem to bloom, to be most truly themselves.

So it was with Dad, but in a bitterly exaggerated way. I caught sight only of the afterglow of his 'floruit'. And after a certain stage that twilight, in its turn, faded so quickly and dramatically for reasons we could not fathom at the time. But, of course, it was the unknown illness from which Dad was by then suffering that, for all the joys we knew at home together, in fact generated anxiety and fear and isolation.

In the last years of Dad's life, as his powers waned so quickly, perhaps some of the happy memories of those years came back to him. Perhaps, deep inside his mind, not everything was lost. That is the hope I nurse.

※

Three faded green report forms tell the story of Dad's 'floruit'.

On those forms, every autumn, the successive commanding officers at Pachmarhi and at Saugor wrote a summary of Dad's work and character. Three pages, from six different officers, cover the eight years' work, from 1932 to 1939. The ink has faded but the writing is clear, and the story is straightforward and brief. The single page that covered the first ten years of Dad's time in India is missing.

At the time of the first three reports, Dad was a sergeant:

[1932] A very reliable and trustworthy NCO. Intelligent, conscientious and thorough in all his work.

[1933] In his work in the carpenter's shop and target store he has shown himself adaptable and resourceful. He carries out his very responsible duties with thoroughness and intelligence. [The maintenance of the weapons ranges and targets for firing practice was central to the work of the school.]

[1934] His work during the last twelve months has

amply confirmed the estimate of his capacities that I made in the preceding year.

Then, after Dad's first six months as RQMS, the commanding officer wrote of him:

> [1935] Has carried out his duties as RQMS very satisfactorily. Has plenty of self-reliance and initiative, and takes a keen interest not only in his work but also in all matters connected with the small arms school. In his dealings with the Indian ranks and followers of the school, he has shown tact and firmness. Has passed the Higher Standard Urdu.

Soon after he was appointed RQMS, Dad began to prepare for his second leave in England. With his higher rate of pay, he increased his savings. He began to buy National Savings certificates, to be redeemed, with interest, in five or ten years' time. Perhaps he was already beginning to think of life after he retired from the Army, or even after the British granted India her independence, a topic much discussed there and in Parliament in the 1930s.

But Dad had his leave to look forward to. He opened savings and deposit accounts with Lloyds Bank especially for the trip Home.

He was saving everything he could. In February 1936 he was able to transfer £1,000 for use back in Cornwall, leaving £238 in his account in India.

More than sixty years later, as I read his bank books, I remembered that when I was a little boy Dad used to say to me, 'Take care of the pennies and the pounds will take care of themselves.' Then, when I was older, he once said to me, very thoughtfully, 'It takes a long time to save a thousand pounds.'

I had no idea then of what he was thinking. Now I saw what those words had really meant. That was the sum that he had saved to take back to Cornwall in 1936. He had done it all for his family. It was for his sisters and then, later, for us that he lived. It was a huge amount of money for a person in his position, and for his family. It is hardly possible to imagine how he had stinted spending on himself in India over the previous years, or how he lavished gifts on the family in Cornwall during his time there that year.

But the most important thing about the family at that time was that none of them was in the grip of Huntington's. Dad's second Home leave took place during a respite for them all.

So, in the summer of 1936, Dad arrived back in Cornwall. He brought with him a new collapsible, accordion-like camera, which years later fascinated me as a little boy. During his time at Home he took many photographs. They show his sisters and their growing families, and him on the beach, wearing one of the modest, long-sleeved swimming costumes of those years. They show the family on walks and making picnics on the Cornish cliffs.

Dad also visited Rene and Florrie and their families in the Midlands and in South Devon. He took Florrie's two eldest sons on a railway excursion to Yelverton, and from there on the winding branch-line to Princetown in the heart of Dartmoor. He showed them some of the photographs that he had taken in India, like those that he used to send them with his letters. They captured vivid scenes of his life there: Dad walking across a river with his boots laced together and hanging around his shoulders; standing on a stepping-stone as the water swirls past him; sitting on a canvas chair outside a large tent on an exercise in the jungle; dressed in a light civilian suit in the garden of a bungalow; standing in his long, white umpire's coat in a formal photograph of the Infantry School's cricket team; a night photograph with silvery streams of fireworks; two tiny tiger cubs; a bear cub; photographs of friends on picnics, with a gramophone, and swimming in the river; and several snaps of Dad's Jack Russell terrier, Tuppy.

At the end of the summer and his leave, Dad returned to Pachmarhi. A little later, in January 1937, he transferred a further £250 to the Penzance branch of Lloyds for the use of the family in Cornwall, as he settled down for the next seven years in India. As it turned out, the War would mean that he would not see England again for eight years.

Dad's reports in those years show that his work and career went from strength to strength, and that he was marked out for further promotion.

> [1936] An excellent RQMS with an intimate knowledge of his work and all Regulations connected with it. His supervision of both British and Indian ranks is good. His knowledge of Urdu, pleasant and outspoken manner, and his wide grasp of all Quarter-Mastering matters warrant his name being placed upon the list of those recommended for a commission in the Indian Army as Quarter-Masters.

> [1937, the same officer as in 1935 and 1936 wrote:] He has maintained throughout 1937 a very high standard of efficiency and it is greatly due to his untiring efforts that the Quarter-Mastering branch of the School is so smoothly run. Has a good knowledge of Urdu, and has controlled both the British and Indian staff with tact

and firmness. Has a wide knowledge of Regulations and Office work. A keen sportsman.

[1938, a new commandant of the school reported:] I entirely concur in the above remarks. He has supervised the Quarter-Mastering branch in an extremely able manner. He is cheerful, resourceful and has plenty of initiative. He has a thorough working command of Urdu, and gets a high standard of efficiency from the staff working under him due to his tact and firmness. He is a warrant-officer in whom I have the utmost trust. I consider him suitable for appointment to the Indian Army as Quarter-Master.

[1939, A further new commandant wrote:] He has maintained his high standard. Under his excellent and very efficient supervision the Quarter-Mastering work of the School has proceeded in a smooth and capable manner. He is tactful, always cheerful, and full of resource and initiative. His handling of the staff under him, both British and Indian, is excellent. An excellent type of warrant-officer.

Just beneath this report Dad has signed his initials, dating his interview with the commanding officer, '22/8', 22nd August. It was the very day on which Molotov, Stalin's foreign minister, on behalf of the Soviet Union, and Ribbentrop, on behalf of Hitler, signed their non-aggression pact. In a secret protocol Stalin and Hitler agreed to divide Central and Eastern Europe between them. War was already inevitable. Stalin's agreement with Hitler made it infinitely more sinister and destructive. That was Stalin's purpose. Hitler attacked Poland on the 1st of September, an attack which Stalin's forces supported, invading Poland from the East, later in the month. Great Britain declared war on Germany in support of Poland on the 3rd of September.

With the coming of war, the Small Arms School moved from Pachmarhi to Saugor. It took over the training school of the Indian cavalry regiments. Pachmarhi became (and remains) the headquarters of the Indian Army Education Corps. For his part in the move to Saugor, Dad received an additional report:

> [15 November 1939] On the recent reorganisation of the Small Arms School, India, this WO has come to the British Wing at Saugor as RQMS, having previously been employed in a similar capacity at Pachmarhi. I most heartily endorse the remarks of the Commandants of the Pachmarhi Wing, extending over a period of many years. He is a WO of the highest character and his work is excellent in every way.

A few months later Dad received his commission as Lieutenant Quartermaster.

He had everything to live for.

7

Commissioned

I REMEMBER Dad's commission. It used to hang in an ebony frame on the wall in my brother's bedroom.

That commission made me feel so proud, but Dad never made any mention of all that he had achieved, having begun life with so little in material terms. Perhaps it was Mum who encouraged him to have it framed.

As he became ill, I remember thinking to myself, 'How is it that Dad who did so much for his country, for all of us, has come to this?' It was a thought to share with no one, not because there was no one but because there is no way truly to share such a feeling that breaks the heart of a child. Anyone who tells you otherwise has no inkling of what it is like. I loved him and this had happened to him. That was everything.

The commission – at first, an Emergency Commission – came to Dad from the 'King Emperor George VI', nine months after the declaration of War. On the 5th of July 1940 he was appointed quartermaster-lieutenant on the list of the First Kumaon Rifles.

As a boy I used to admire Dad's smart regimental tie, with its green and red stripes, which I now wear at reunions in England. In October 2003 I was honoured to wear it at the Regiment's reunion at its centre at Ranikhet in the Kumaon, not far from India's borders with China and Nepal, and to lay a wreath at the memorial there in honour of those who had served in the Regiment and died in the service of their country. Dad was very close to me there during the silence that we observed.

Dad's service book shows that, when his commission was signed in July 1940, he had served 24 years and 83 days altogether with the DCLI: two years and 319 days in Great Britain and Ireland, and 21 years and 129 days (more than half his life) in India. For all the recommendations going back to the mid 1930s that he should be commissioned, Dad, like many others, finally received this opportunity and responsibility sooner than it might have come, because of the War. He was well prepared.

※

Sixty years on from the date of his receiving it, I showed an Indian friend from church Dad's Emergency Commission, confirmed as 'regular' two and a half years later in the document that was to hang in due course on the wall in my brother's bedroom. Maurice had been a Colonel in the Indian Army until his retirement in the 1990s. By an odd coincidence, he was born on the day in 1940 on which Dad was commissioned. Like Dad, he was a devout Christian.

Maurice's eyes began to shine as he read the document. It was, he told me, drafted in more or less the same words as those used, since Independence, by the President of India. Nowadays the words are printed in English on one side of the paper, and given in the officer's vernacular language on the reverse.

Maurice paused on the line referring to the King's 'trust and confidence in your Loyalty, Courage and good Conduct.' With pride and a burst of joy he said to me, 'It feels exactly like that – the responsibility to behave like that.'

Dad's feelings, I am sure, were the same. We saw that it was so, even near the end of his life in hospital, when he always stood straight with head held high as the National Anthem was played on the television in the ward.

※

It must have been curious for Dad to be commissioned as an officer after serving so long in the ranks and as a warrant officer. After some time as quartermaster he became the administrative officer at the British Wing, working for the Commandant of the Small Arms School. He helped organise courses for many 'squads' of subalterns sent out from England. As the war gathered pace in the Far East as well as in Europe, a stream of young officers passed through Saugor on training courses, many of them to be sent on to serve in the Middle East or Burma.

These young officers were, for the most part, twenty years younger than Dad, and many of them were accustomed to a life at Home unlike anything that he had experienced there. In *A Shaft of Sunlight*, his memoir of life in India in the 1930s and 1940s, Philip Mason, who worked closely with the Indian Army during his time in the Indian civil service, wrote:

There was one Major who had risen from the ranks; 'Nice young men,' he confided in me one day, 'but not very serious.'

For all the differences in background, age and experience of life, Dad's fellow officers respected and liked him, and he them. In later years Dad used to speak warmly of a string of them, names which lodged themselves in my memory: Colonel 'Tug' Thornton, Colonel George Stobart, Colonel Grant Taylor, Colonel Orr, Colonel Forteath, Major Guy Stringer and Major Stacey, from many of whom cards used to arrive each Christmas in the 1950s.

There was the padre at Saugor, the Reverend Tony Lawrance whose wife Mary died in India. Dad used to tend her grave after Tony's return to England. Years later, when he remarried, Tony Lawrance wished Dad to be his best man, but it was not to be. For a while they had been out of touch with each other because of moving house. A little after the wedding, when they had re-established contact, the Lawrances came to North Devon on holiday from their Rectory in Yorkshire – this was in 1952 – and Tony Lawrance gave us a puppy, 'Patch', from his English bull-terrier bitch.

Another of Dad's close friends was 'Nobby' Clark, who was also commissioned from among the warrant-officers at about the same time as Dad; Dad was godfather to his daughter, Georgina.

In July 1943, exactly three years after he was commissioned, Dad was promoted Captain; then, Acting Major in October 1943, and Temporary Major in January 1944 as the 'admin officer' at the Small Arms School. Sixty years later I met another Major who had served at Saugor. He and his wife had lived in a bungalow only about fifty yards away from Dad and Mum in Haig Road. He told me that Dad was by then number two or three to Colonel Gray, the Commanding Officer at the school.

Everything was going well.

8
Matchmaking

IN JULY 1944, six months after he was promoted Major, Dad was visited at Saugor by Charlie Paul, his brother-in-law, Florrie's husband.

Charlie was a sergeant in the Royal Engineers. He was working in a railway operating company, as an instructor. His job was to teach men how to drive steam engines. Before the war he had still been a fireman, the driver's junior colleague on the footplate of steam engines, stoking up the fire to heat the boiler. In 1945 he had to return to that less well paid role on the Great Western Railway (GWR) until he gained afresh the promotion that he had won in the Sappers.

Charlie had come out from England via Ceylon (now Sri Lanka) and was travelling from Madras to Burma to join the campaign against Japan. He was granted permission to visit Dad on a short leave, and at 2pm on Monday, 24th July, Dad met Charlie at the height of the monsoon. It was raining as they met.

※

I have on my desk Dad's diary and notebooks for 1944. He was forty-two years old. It was the year when the

Allies closed in for the kill on Germany, advancing relentlessly through Poland, Italy and France. It was the year when Dad was allowed to take his delayed home leave in England. It was the year when Dad met Mum.

And this diary seems to me to be holy ground. It means so much to me not only because it is Dad's own personal record, in his hand, then still clear, elegant and firm. It is holy because it comes from the year that crowned all his successes.

It is holy for me, too, because of the way the story ended for Dad – and for his sisters, Clara and Kathleen; how it ended or will end or may end for all of us caught up in this dance, this chorea of St Vitus, from which there is no escape. But for a while, in 1944, all looked well for Dad and his sisters. For the moment no one in their family was affected by that horror, no one was ill. And I know that, whatever came later, when I understood it so poorly and made such mistakes, I am lucky that Dad was my father.

※

'Still raining,' Dad recorded that evening before going to bed. 'Had a good drink of beer and a bit of roast beef – what a chat we had about Home, too.'

Charlie later wrote to Florrie and his children to tell them that Dad had arranged for him to be treated 'like royalty' during his time at Saugor.

And that was the evening when Uncle Charlie told Dad about Mum, and played the role of matchmaker. Short and stocky, with a dark Cornish complexion and thick black hair, down-to-earth, astute and full of common sense, Uncle Charlie was an unlikely candidate for this role.

Of course, Florrie must have taken the lead, for she and her sisters were concerned about their brother, who was surely lonely at times. One of his close colleagues and friends died that year, in middle age; and Dad's dog 'Tuppy', a Jack Russell terrier, also died. Dad's concern, too, for his fellow-officers' children is clear in the diary. He wished that Georgina, his goddaughter, could leave Saugor during the intense heat in the August of that summer, when he visited the grave of her stillborn brother at Pachmarhi. He was there to conduct an inspection of the cantonment, the first time since 1939 that he had been able to visit his 'spiritual home' in the hills. He told Georgina's father, Nobby Clark, how much he wanted children of his own.

Perhaps it was the implausibility of Charlie's acting as a matchmaker, his solid reliability, which gave his words about Mum special force with Dad. About fifteen years later I occasionally met Uncle Charlie on the bus that I used to catch to school. He would be on his way to join a slightly unusual shift at the railway junction and marshalling yard to begin his day's work; it was not his regular bus. Uncle Charlie was always very kind to me. Perhaps there was something almost tender in his rugged look, well camouflaged by his engine driver's uniform and cap, smudged with Welsh coal, that said, 'But for my visit to Saugor in July 1944 to tell Jack about Grace, you would not be here.' And I recall how, on one of those mornings, he encouraged me to persevere in my studies, as he made his way past me along the gangway of the upper deck of the bus, with its notice enjoining 'No Spitting'.

On their second day together at Saugor Dad took Charlie for a walk around the ranges of the weapons school. They also went to see the farm and vegetable gardens that he managed. He kept sketches of the vegetable plots and lists of the names of the workers in his notebook.

Together, Dad and Charlie wrote letters Home to Florrie, Jack (Charlie's second son) and Kathleen, who was doing war-work at a factory in Gloucestershire which produced aircraft propellers. It was still raining as Dad and Charlie wrote. Already some forty inches had fallen since the monsoon had started – 'very good rains indeed', Dad noted.

To round off the visit, Herbert and Jessie, friends with whom Dad sometimes stayed the night after the cinema show at the Club on Saturday evenings, visited Dad and met Charlie. They brought their children with them. Then Charlie set off from Saugor to resume his journey to the frontier with Burma.

※

What was it about Mum – Grace, as Charlie spoke about her – that engaged Dad's interest? Her photographs from those years supply a ready answer, and surely Florrie had thoughtfully given Charlie some snaps to take to Saugor.

Then, Grace had recently been freed from the responsibility of caring for her father and mother who had died in 1939 and 1943. She was still keeping house for her two bachelor brothers, Jack and George, rather against their inclination and certainly with little by way of thanks from them, but her mother's death the previous year left an enormous gap in her life that was aching to be filled.

But there was something else about her that I heard from a detached observer, who, in those years, watched Grace's family from a house across the road in Plympton and came to know them well after the War. She told me that she could tell that there was what she called 'something special' about Grace. She sensed an integrity and selfless loyalty. In part this showed itself in Mum's religious faith, which went beyond the rather routine Sunday observance of some in her family.

One way or another, Dad would have asked Charlie about this. From his diary you can see how much his faith mattered to him. Week by week he noted that he attended church on Sunday mornings and evenings, for matins and evensong. Often he also attended the early morning service of Holy Communion. Sometimes (for example on 4th June, Trinity Sunday that year), he records that he received the elements of the Communion, the bread wafer and the wine, although he had not yet been confirmed by a bishop.

The padre, Tony Lawrance, had done much to encourage Dad's faith. On 16th July, Dad records: 'Church 7pm. I read the lesson – the first time in my life.' It was Tony Lawrance who offered Dad the privilege of receiving the Holy Communion before he was confirmed; this must have been very rare indeed in the Anglican Church in those days. Perhaps it was shyness about this that once prompted him to turn back when, on his way to St Peter's, he spotted that the commanding officer, Brigadier Cameron, was going there for the early service.

In September Tony Lawrance accompanied Dad to

Jubbalpore where, on the sixth of the month, 'I was confirmed by the Bishop of Nagpur at 18.30 in the Garrison church.'

Two years later this Bishop, Alec Hardie, stayed with Dad at his bungalow in Saugor. By then Mum had arrived in India, bringing me with her. Bishop Hardie allowed me to play a little with his hunter pocket watch, and commented to Mum that her son was a 'fine baby', so making a friend of her for life.

In the year that India became independent the Bishop wrote warmly of Dad as a person 'for whom I have the highest regard' and who had 'done more for the church in Saugor than any layman I have known there during the nine years in which I have been bishop of this diocese'. He refers to Dad as 'Church Secretary at Saugor'.

So when Charlie mentioned that Grace was confirmed and regularly went to Holy Communion, it surely rang a bell with Dad.

※

Forty-five years later Judy, my wife, and I bought a cottage in East Sussex.

Mum was staying with us in London at the time of her birthday at the end of October. Judy was at work but I had a day off from the office, so Mum and I went to see the cottage a few weeks before we took possession of it. It was a golden autumn afternoon. The sun shone warmly in a slightly hazy blue sky. In the gardens the first bonfires of the season were giving out plumes of grey-white smoke from barrow-loads of fallen leaves.

We arrived at the cottage in the middle of the afternoon. It has a fine view along a wide valley in the Weald. Towards evening the sky over the valley often seems to reflect the light of the sea, fifteen miles away.

As Mum caught her first glimpse of the house, she said: 'It's a gentleman's residence'. Then she added, 'Wouldn't Dad have loved it here? And keeping a few chickens ...'?

Her first comment was far from the truth, in the conventional sense. The cottage had been built for a farm labourer's family in 1932, although, as Thackeray knew, there is no reason why a labourer should be any the less a gentleman than those who used to be accorded that title in this world. But Mum's second comment was exactly right. Dad surely would have loved it here. Often, when I am working on the vegetable plot, I think of that.

The task of managing the smallholding that he showed to Charlie was more than just a job for Dad. The diagrams which he made carefully in 1945 to plan the crops to be grown that year, with the names of the Indian workers tending the separate parts of the holding, somehow show that. He kept them in his personal notebook. In his diary Dad also recorded, at various times, that he had had a rabbit hutch built; that some ducklings had hatched; that some cattle had arrived at Saugor. The farm was not a big part of his job, but he enjoyed it as an escape from the office.

A few years later, when I was three years old, we were living in a bungalow at St Ives in Cornwall. It is my second memory. Dad and I are together in our back garden: I am 'helping' him clean out the chicken house and their exercise pen. Wearing corduroy trousers, a jersey and his old trilby hat, Dad is stirring, in a dixie (Urdu for cooking pot), the mash with which he will feed the fowls.

'Be careful, John, that's hot.'

'It isn't hot, Daddy, 'cos I eated a bit.'

When one of our chickens died, or was somehow taken by a fox, he told me that it had flown away to Land's End, where I loved playing on the cliffs. All would be well at Land's End; all would be well.

He was such a gentle, tender-hearted, faithful, reliable, wise man. I am lucky that Uncle Charlie visited him at Saugor.

※

Soon after Dad had seen Charlie off from Saugor to rejoin his unit, he had to decide when to take the Home leave that had been delayed by the War.

9
Home Leave

ONE DAY AT THE END of July 1944 Dad recorded, 'Not feeling too well – a touch of tummy trouble in the evening.' In fact, his medical notes show that the doctor diagnosed that he was suffering from mild dysentery. A few days later he received a letter from Charlie, by then diverted to Julandar, now Jullundur, in the Punjab, where, at Amritsar, he visited the Sikhs' Golden Temple.

The Allies' victories and advance in Europe now made it possible for Dad to be released for Home leave. It would mean an absence from Saugor of three and a half months in all. Dad noted that there was 'a chance to go Home – but I'll wait until the summer [of 1945].'

He was longing to see England again. The previous October he had copied out Shakespeare's words on a sheet of writing paper to keep beside him (King Richard the Second, II, i, 42ff).

While the offer of Home leave was still on the table, Dad visited Pachmarhi and inspected the station where he had worked so happily for ten years. Then, on his return to Saugor at the end of August, he wrote in his diary: 'Sent in my name for leave in September!'

> INFANTRY SCHOOL.
> SAUGOR.
> C.P.
> INDIA.
>
> *This England*
>
> This other Eden, demi-paradise,
> This fortress, built by nature for herself,
> Against infection & the hand of
> war — This happy breed of men,
> this little world,
> This precious stone set in the silver sea,
> Which serves it in the office of a wall,
> or as a moat defensive to a house,
> Against the envy of less happier
> lands
> This blessed plot — this earth,
> this realm, this England.

Dad began to 'prepare his boxes' for home. He wrote to his sister Clara at Madron near Penzance and told her that he was coming. On 2nd September, the eve of the fifth anniversary of the British declaration of war on Germany, he recorded: 'The news from Home is marvellous. Our troops crossed the Belgian border at 11.00 hours today.' The next day was declared by the King to be a Day of Thanksgiving, and, at St Peter's church, 'there was a good congregation. Guy [Stringer, his old friend] took the collection with me.' Dad's confirmation at Jubbalpore took place three days later.

On 16th September Dad received the details of his travel home 'via Deolali', and he was 'very busy packing up'. He left Saugor on the eighteenth, and sailed from

Bombay on the twenty-seventh. The journey by way of the Suez Canal, which took twenty-seven days, amounted to some 6,260 miles, according to his atlas, in which he had been marking the Allies' progress in Europe since D-Day. He arrived in England, probably at Liverpool, on 24th October. He travelled by train to Devon and stayed with Florrie in Plympton for a few days before moving on to Penzance.

※

At the end of her life, lying in her bed in hospital but with her mind and powerful memory still clear and reliable, Mum told me of her first glimpse of Dad in Plympton. She was working upstairs at home, making the beds for Jack and George.

'I looked out of the bedroom window, and there he was, walking along with Florrie's children, so handsome and tall, and he looked so nice.'

It was 28th October, a Saturday. After walking from Florrie and Charlie's house along Stone Barton to Plympton station, the route which gave Mum the chance to catch that sight of them, Dad 'went up to Dartmoor with Jack, Doris and Coulson'.

On Sunday Dad attended a service at St Mary's church with Terry, Florrie's eldest son. Mum was probably in the congregation at that service. It was her thirty-fifth birthday.

The next morning Dad caught the train to Penzance. He went to stay with Clara and her husband Charlie Semmens. He wrote and underlined:

<u>Very nice to be Home again</u>.

Kathleen arrived on leave from her war-work, 'looking very well'.

On Wednesday Dad 'went over to Newlyn to see them all'. On Thursday he visited 'town [Penzance] with Clara and Charlie', and took Kathleen to a meal at the Ritz Hotel there. At around this date the set lunch at an excellent hotel in the West of England cost four shillings (20p):

> Vegetable soup
> Fried fillet of plaice with anchovy sauce
> Roast lamb or Cold Buffet
> Apple tart – thick cream
> Cheese and biscuits
> Dessert

On Saturday Dad 'went to Newlyn for the fish'. He loved fresh fish, just caught in the sea on which his family had worked for generations. How he must have longed for it in India. On Sunday he attended St Peter's church, Newlyn, at 11am and 6pm, just as he and his sisters had done for so long as children.

The weather was changeable, but one day Dad went for a walk to Morvah, Pendeen (where Florrie had been in service twenty years earlier), St Just and Land's End. It was a march of at least twenty miles. He arrived home by 6pm after a late start because it had been raining in the morning. He was very fit. Next, he spent a day with Nora and her husband Reg.

The routine of family events continued until the middle of the month, with teas together, church, and a visit to the cinema to see *For Whom The Bell Tolls*. On his last day with the family he enjoyed another long walk, from Penzance to Sancreed and back 'by 14.15 hours'.

On the day after that walk Dad went by train to Southampton to stay with his old friends, John and Emma, who had retired to England from India a little while earlier. It took nine hours to reach Southampton from Penzance, and the weather was 'very cold' throughout Dad's two days there. John introduced him to his sister – perhaps in an attempt at matchmaking. Kathleen, too, had sent him a photograph of herself and two friends with whom she worked in the factory; 'the three glamour girls', she wrote on the back.

On 18th November Dad made another nine-hour journey, to his sister Rene and her husband Harold in Bushbury, a couple of miles north of Wolverhampton. Rene met him at the station. 'All looking well,' he wrote. Their daughter, Megan, fourteen years old at the time, recalls Dad arriving in his uniform at their house in Kipling Road. She remembers his 'lovely dark grey eyes' and sunburnt complexion and moustache. Her brother Graham, then eleven years old, remembers him as a 'lovely, kind uncle', with an upright, military bearing. Dad was interested in the linnet and greenfinch that Rene kept, and every evening he carefully covered the birdcage to enable them to roost peacefully and have a good sleep. He used to do just the same for our two successive canaries in the 1950s.

While he was staying with Rene, Dad went to Stone in Staffordshire for a day: 'a grand day with Guy Stringer's people. Home by 9pm.' He visited Harold's family, the Corfields, and 'Maria' for tea; Rene was probably matchmaking this time. He took Rene to the cinema to see *Dr Wassal* – 'bed 00.45' – on Friday, and a play, *Nothing but the Truth*, on Saturday.

On both his Sundays at Rene's he went to church. On the first, Rene came to meet him after the service – he wrote in his diary that in the service they had sung *Jesus Shall Reign*, a favourite hymn of his. On the second Sunday he went to the local church in Bushbury in the morning and to St Peter's, the parish church of Wolverhampton, in the evening. By the second Sunday, 26th November, he was again finding the weather 'very cold'.

On Monday morning Dad left for Plymouth. The journey took twelve and a half hours. At North Road station, his nephew Jack met him and took him back to Florrie and Charlie's. Kathleen was also staying there for a couple of days. Dad took her to Plymouth to have a portrait photograph taken. It is a beautiful picture, which, as it turned out, caught her calm grace and gentle features just in time. Within a year or two her mind and body, and with them the peace you can sense in her expression in that photograph, would begin to be destroyed by Huntington's.

In Plympton there were more family outings. Dad went on a walk with his nephew Jack through Plymbridge woods to Roborough, a village on the edge of Dartmoor.

He took Florrie, her daughter Doris, and Florrie's best friend, Hilda (Mum's elder sister), to see The White Cliffs of Dover at the cinema. This popular film was based on the verses of the American poet Alice Duer Miller. She had died in 1942, having caught in her poetry, from the point of view of an 'outsider', as she depicted her heroine, something of what enabled her adopted country to survive those years and, finally, achieve victory:

I have loved England, dearly and deeply,
Since the first morning, shining and pure ...
When they pointed 'the white cliffs of Dover',
Startled, I found there were tears on my cheek ...

The tree of liberty grew and changed and spread,
But the seed was English ...
In a world where England is finished and dead,
I do not wish to live.

On Sunday, Dad travelled to Totnes to visit a friend, Frank, and stayed the night. He went to church there on Sunday morning and arrived 'Home again by 3pm'.

On Monday, 4th December, Dad and Mum met for the first time. They walked together to Lee Moor, a village on the southern fringe of Dartmoor.

It was the start of their courtship.

10
Interlude

FIFTY-TWO YEARS LATER Mum lies on a Pegasus air mattress in a side room off Ward 12 in Mount Gould Hospital in Plymouth. The electric motor of an air-compressor hums very quietly and, every so often, it gently inflates or deflates one or another of the lungs of the mattress. The 'Friends of Ward 12' have raised the money for the hospital to buy more of these mattresses. Ward 12 is a special place. It has many grateful friends. The flow of air changes the contours of the bed and reduces the risk of bedsores. Mum was already suffering from one when she was moved to the specialist unit here from a ward in a general hospital.

Outside, about sixty feet from the window of her little room, stands an immense horse chestnut tree, covered in fresh green leaves. The first white and saffron flowers are opening. Mum watched the tree's leaves turn brown and fall, along with the conkers, last autumn. She saw the tree's branches bare against the blue winter sky.

Mum has lain on this bed for six months. Every two hours or so, she is turned from one side to the other by members of a group of skilled and dedicated nurses and assistants. She is paralysed on her left side, the effect of the stroke that she suffered in September. She cannot feed or clean herself.

Mum's speech is a little slow, soft but clear. Sometimes her mind is muddled, but often it is completely lucid. Sometimes she sleeps deeply, sometimes fitfully. After a deep sleep this morning, her mind is alert.

'Dad was lovely, wasn't he?' she says. 'I've been over nearly all of it now. I'm happy.'

11
Dear Octopus

MUM'S FAMILY WAS POOR; nothing like as hard-pressed as Dad and his sisters during their childhood and youth, but poor nevertheless. She told me that when she was helping her mother keep house in the 1920s and 1930s and they were dusting and sweeping together, she used to take up a piece of coconut matting in the little back drawing-room in order to clean the floor. There was no carpet in the family home, number 7, Stone Barton, in those days. There never was, except for special occasions when they borrowed one. Many families lived like that.

Mum was born in October 1909 into a large, united family. Descended from generations of farm labourers and gamekeepers, her parents, Henry and Agnes, and many of her uncles and aunts had served as butlers and valets, cooks and maids during the sixty-three years of Queen Victoria's reign.

In 1895 at the age of twenty-eight they married in London.

Both of them had been in service. On her mother's side of the family, the Alderseys, it had begun with Mum's grandfather and grandmother. By the 1840s they had been drawn to London to find work.

Young people were by then no longer needed in such numbers to work on the land, especially after the abolition of the Corn Laws and the fall in prices that followed the loss of the protection that they gave. Cereals gave way to cattle and sheep. The wages of farm labourers fell. London was growing quickly and on a great scale. Because of the fruits of the industrial revolution and of Great Britain's trade with her Empire and the rest of the world, the middle classes were growing richer. In the capital and in other big towns demand grew for domestic servants.

Like tens of thousands of others, Mum's grandparents found their way to London to earn their living. After a time there as domestic servants they moved back to their rural roots in Nottinghamshire. In 1866 Mum's mother, Agnes, was born. Agnes' father was by then working there as a gamekeeper on an estate. The Aldersey family continued to have a strong sense of belonging to the land. That feeling never left them or their descendants.

About twenty years later, in her turn, Agnes moved to London. She earned her living as a kitchen-maid and, with experience and training, as a cook.

For a while Agnes served the Prince and Princess of Wales in their household at Marlborough House. At that time her hair was jet-black and her fellow servants called her 'The Raven'. Once, running through the corridors of the building from the servants' hall to serve in the dining room, Agnes met the Prince. He stopped her and asked why she was running. She explained that the servants had little time to finish their own food before serving him and his guests at table. After that encounter the times of the meals were changed to give the servants time to eat properly before meals were served 'upstairs'.

After her adventures at Marlborough House, with visits to Sandringham with the Royal family at Christmas, Agnes went to work as head cook for a family in Putney. It was there that she met Henry Jarrold, her future husband, serving as valet in the same house.

Henry was born in 1867. His family gave him a much harsher start in life than Agnes' had given her. Afterwards, however, he was to find himself unusually blessed in his marriage and in the family that he and his wife would produce and cherish.

Henry's father, Elijah, had moved from Stowmarket in Suffolk to work as a builder's labourer in London in the 1860s. His wife, Emma, died in childbirth when she was only twenty-eight years old. Elijah became a heavy drinker and remarried. He sadistically bullied the children of his first marriage. He threw Henry out of the house when he was a boy of only seven.

Henry somehow found his way from London to York. He was brought up and educated there in a school for orphans run by a lady called Miss Milner. He remained devoted to her memory all his life. He went into service as a 'boots boy'. He did well. In the next few years, as a valet and later a butler, Henry sometimes travelled to Ireland and Scotland in the summer and to the South of France and Corfu in the winter. When she heard them as a young girl, Mum was fascinated by the tales of his journeys on the Continent with his 'gentleman's family'.

After their marriage in 1895 Henry and Agnes had eight children. With Mum's arrival in 1909, they completed their family – five sons and three daughters.

During those fourteen years they were often on the move around England, in service with various families, first in Yorkshire, and later in Worcestershire and the West of England.

After service at Tehidy House in Cornwall, where Mum was born, and not long after King George V came to the throne in 1910, the family moved to Plymouth. For two years Henry and Agnes kept a sweetshop there but they could not make it pay. According to Mum, her parents were too generous to the local children as well as their own. Perhaps it was as a toddler, in the sweetshop, that Mum gained her life-long taste for liquorice and chocolate.

In 1912 they moved to Plympton St Mary, five miles east of Plymouth, where Mum's father once more earned his living as a butler, first for the Strode family at Newnham House, and afterwards for the families at Hemerdon House and Cann House, Tamerton Foliot.

The ten Jarrolds lived in a terraced house with three bedrooms at number 12, Moorland View (later re-named and re-numbered as 24, Moorland Avenue). It is to this house that Mum's first memories relate.

'The first thing I remember was being in the back lane of our row of houses, a bit lonely as all the other children had gone in a horse-and-wagon on the chapel outing to the seaside at Wembury,' Mum told me.

'My next memory was of one breakfast-time, jumping up when Mother was making my cocoa, knocking a kettle of water over my shoulders. All the family rushed around frantically trying to help poor Mother. The district nurse came and did my wound. I lay in a cot in the kitchen, being spoiled once more. Mother slept on a mattress on the floor by my cot for a few nights.'

Mum always looked at her parents through rose-tinted spectacles. 'I can't help doing it,' she told me. But her memories contain nuggets that run counter to the way she wished to see things. The stories that she passed on reveal that she had a formidable power of recall and was an honest witness. Her memories have always proved to be accurate when it has been possible to check them.

※

Mum started school on the thirty-first of August 1914, one day short of four weeks after the First World War broke out, and two months before her fifth birthday.

'Starting school was a shock to me, being the youngest of eight and a bit spoiled by the others. My sister Hilda was ten years older than me and had already left school. She took me to the baby school, called Bridge School in those days, at the foot of Station Hill. She told me to run home, and told Mother that she hadn't been able to catch me. The next day Mother took me, and, very tearfully clutching a packet of chocolate drops, I was left with Mrs Bettes and Miss Blight...

'Our house in Moorland View was lovely. A few weeks later at Christmas, it was filled with holly and ivy, and we just had stockings filled with simple presents, and oranges, apples, and nuts. We had a lovely Christmas dinner and Christmas pudding (set alight with brandy), with ten of us around the table. Two doors away lived my friend, Edie Law, and we always had a good Christmas, with our dolls and toys...

'We had baths on Saturdays in a tin bath in front of the kitchen fire; there was no bathroom there. After the bath we had sweets.'

Sixty years later, out of the blue, Mum received two visitors.

'Yesterday was a strange day. I answered the doorbell. A lady and a gentleman stood there, and the lady said, 'Can you tell us where to find 14 Moorland View where I used to live?' I gave a shout, 'Edie Law!' and she said, 'Grace Jarrold!' We had not met for sixty years. She was my playmate. They came in and had cups of tea and coconut buns (I didn't have anything else). They stayed two and a half hours and we talked the hind leg off a donkey, about all the games that we played and of the people we knew. They live in Bristol. Edie's husband was tickled pink at our meeting. It was very funny after all those years.'

Another of Mum's friends in Moorland View was Edie Paul. At school Edie was a lively pupil. Like her brother Bill, Edie had the bluest eyes that Mum ever saw. Once, the teacher tried to get her to concentrate, saying 'Edith Paul, put on your thinking-cap.' Edie replied, 'I can't, Miss; I've only got my 'shanter'.

※

During Mum's first years at school her two eldest brothers were in the Army, serving on the Western Front of the Great War against Imperial Germany in France.

'I remember Mother crying when Harry and Jack went to war. When they came back from the front on leave their uniforms were filthy from the mud of the trenches and full of fleas. Mother used matches to get the fleas to jump out of the serge; the cloth was so thick and that was the only way to get rid of them.'

After the United States entered the Great War two Americans were billeted with her family for several months in late 1917 and 1918. Mum was frightened of them because they used to play boisterously with her, throwing her up into the air and catching her. 'Yanks', as she often called them, rather fondly, always amused her by their 'exuberance', a favourite word of hers.

Food was short. According to the log-book kept by the headmaster of the senior school, called Geasons, his staff and pupils used to grow an annual crop of potatoes during the War and for a good few years after it, partly for food and partly to teach the children how to work a vegetable garden. The area under cultivation at the school in 1917 was seven and three quarter roods, a plot that amounts to almost two acres. In the spring of that year Geasons' staff and pupils planted a hundredweight of seed potatoes.

A series of small events and treats marked the passing of each term. In the late spring and summer months the parish church of St Mary, and the Wesleyan and Congregationalist chapels in Ridgeway, as the high street was called, used to organise teas and outings for the children of the village. On those days the schools would be closed.

Not far from the school stood Hillside House where General and Mrs Birdwood lived for many years. They offered Geasons great support. In early summer each year they gave a tea party for the children in their large garden, with its forest of shrubs and rhododendrons. The wisteria would be in full bloom, covering the south front of the house.

Mr Baple, the energetic new headmaster, recorded in his log-book on the morning of Empire Day, the 24th of May 1917, that 'Suitable lessons were given and General Birdwood gave a brief address to the children on "The Empire and the Flag".' In the words of the writer of a current textbook,

> The British Empire ... stretches over the whole globe ... The sun never sets or rises over the British dominions ... It would be perfectly possible to put round the earth a girdle of telegraphic wire, the ends of which should rest only upon land that belongs to the British Empire.

Another recent popular history for children told 'Our Empire Story.'

The pride felt in our country's history and achievements was combined with humour and a sense of proportion. On the same day that General Birdwood gave the pupils his talk on the Empire, Mr Baple noted in his log that there was 'a small attendance of children in the afternoon, a circus being in Plympton'.

The following year on St George's Day, the twenty-third of April, there were lessons 'suitable to the day'. A collection in the school raised £1 0s 3d, for the RSPCA's fund for horses wounded in the War, then in its final months.

Plympton St Mary was a loyal, quiet village. It was home to three or four thousand people, including those living in the neighbouring smaller villages of Plympton St Maurice and Colebrook and in the outlying hamlets. There was a spirit of patriotism in the village and school, and of long-suffering, stoical humanity and realism, with modest pleasures and no luxuries; a gentle and patient people, hardy and decent, facing so many hardships together.

Even those on the fringes of society in Mum's childhood seemed to share in this powerful ideal as much as anyone else.

Tramps were sometimes seen passing through Plympton on the main road between Exeter and Plymouth. Without irony, they were known as 'gentlemen of the road'. One of them regularly called on Mum's family. Her mother would give him tea, some food to take on his way and a pair of boots saved up for his visit. Sitting at the kitchen table, he used to tell Mum and her mother of his adventures on his long walk between John o'Groats and Land's End. Even when she was elderly, perhaps partly as a result of this friendship, which lasted for many years, Mum used to carry some loose change with her in her mackintosh pocket in case she met a tramp 'in need of a cup of tea'.

Old-fashioned gypsy caravans sometimes visited the village. Once in a while they made an encampment in the field beside the Tory Brook, between St Mary's church and the livestock market. Fascinated by the sight, the village children watched them cooking on their camp-fires and putting their children to bed under the stars. When one of the gypsies died, he was sent on his way by a large congregation at a funeral service in St Mary's.

In the autumn of 1918 as the Great War was coming to its end, an influenza epidemic (known as 'Spanish 'flu') began to rage in the country. In Plympton only sixty per cent of the children were able to attend school on some days. At the end of October and in early November Mr Baple closed the school completely for a fortnight. One boy, Robert Parsons, died. The pupils brought in their pennies for a wreath; £1 6s 11d was collected. Later they made a contribution to the costs of his funeral.

The following summer the country marked its slow but steady return to normal life on 'Peace Day', the 19th of July. Beacons were lit on hills at traditional sites. Mum's school held a special celebration. She won a prize in the sports which took place in Geasons field. The next day, according to Mr Baple's notes, 'the cake remaining from the festivities was distributed among the children'.

'At the King's express desire', the midsummer holiday was extended from four to five weeks that year. The country, including the children, could begin to breathe more easily for a while.

That summer Mum's brother, Walter, three years her senior, won a scholarship to Corporation Grammar School at North Road in Plymouth. Plympton Grammar School had been closed in the early nineteenth century. It was re-opened in 1921, too late for Wally, so his amily had the additional expense of his train fares to Plymouth every day. He was a clever boy, and the only member of the family to go to grammar school. The Jarrolds had just enough money to pay for the uniform and books that he needed. Mum's father was working as the butler at Newnham House, a mile outside the village. He earned 23 shillings a week (£1 15p). Apart from Wally, Mum's brothers and sisters were by now in work.

In September Wally took up his scholarship. Mum moved up the hill from Bridge School to Geasons. There were about three hundred children at the school, 135 of them boys and 154 girls.

Mum's family bought her new clothes for the move

to the senior school: a warm winter coat, a hat and gloves, and leather lace-up boots. Winters were usually severe and long, and Mum always suffered from chilblains.

'I remember going up to the Big School. I really loved it when I got used to it, especially when I got older, although I went up the hill from the baby school shaking in my shoes on the first day.'

At the end of October the pupils subscribed £1 2s 10d for a portrait of Nurse Edith Cavell. The matron of a hospital in Brussels at the start of the War, Nurse Cavell had become a popular heroine. She had risked her life by helping two hundred British and Allied soldiers to escape to The Netherlands after the German army occupied Belgium in 1914. She was executed by the Germans in 1915. Her picture was placed in the school's main assembly room.

On the eleventh of November 1919, the first national commemoration of the anniversary of the Armistice, Mr Baple wrote in his diary:

> An Assembly was held in the Schoolroom, in accordance with the King's desire. Silence at 11am for a few minutes; then an address on the subject of the day – the Armistice, its results, the League of Nations, etc. School closed in the afternoon.

At the end of the winter, in early 1920, Bridge and Geasons Schools were inspected by His Majesty's Inspectorate of Education. The Inspector reported:

> The discipline, which during the war years at times showed unsteadiness, is now much improved and the staff more settled than it was. The majority of the children are bright and intelligent, though there are a

few very dull ones who seem to need special attention. The subjects of instruction as seen at the time of the visit appear on the whole to be up to the average, and the methods of teaching are generally suitable, although this is more characteristic of the upper than the lower part of the school.

It is clear that the organisation might be improved in certain details which were discussed with the Head Master at the time of the inspection, and the timetable which has been in use a long time needs revision. The scheme of work, which was drawn up some years ago, is too vague and general in character to be of much help to the assistant teachers, and the terminal examinations might well cover a wider range of subjects.

In a school of this size, the children in Standard VII [thirteen-year-olds] should attempt more advanced work by means of private study instead of, as at present, working with Standard VI and occasionally Standard V.

Althia Birdwood countersigned the report of the inspection on behalf of the governors.

By now Mum had just passed her tenth birthday. She had a little less than four years' schooling ahead of her. There were about forty-five children in her class. Mum loved school and worked hard at her lessons.

Perhaps as a result of the inspector's report the school began to arrange for more of its pupils to sit the scholarship examination for the grammar school.

Mum did well in her studies. 'When I was thirteen, I was made head girl, and every morning at eleven o'clock I used to fetch Mr Baple his coffee on a tray from the cottage in Station Road where he and Mrs Baple lived.'

Mr Baple encouraged Mum's parents to put her in for a scholarship to the grammar school. Nothing came of his idea. There was not enough money for the family to buy Mum the uniform and everythiing else that she would have needed for the extra two years at the grammar school to take her school certificate.

'I didn't have the nerve to go in for the scholarship although Mr Baple told me that I could easily pass. I wasn't brave enough – too babyish, I expect. My family was too nice to me; I can't get away from that – they spoilt me.'

Mum always looked back to her days at school with Mr Baple with affection. In 1976, when she was reading the *Devon Life* magazine, she told me: 'I saw a letter by my old schoolmaster, Mr W.H. Baple. He asked pupils of 1919 to 1923 to write to him. I have done so and eagerly await a reply. He says that he has been in India. I told him all the news and hope that he will enjoy reading about my time in India with Dad. You cannot believe the thrill I got from seeing his name.'

Mum would have done well at the grammar school. She never gave the slightest hint of resenting her loss. Even with most of her brothers and sisters already at work, she could see that her family's funds were short. Our country's national income declined by a fifth between 1918 and 1922, and did not recover to the level of 1918 until 1934. The whole period of 1914 to 1934 saw no improvement in the people's standard of living.

So it was not surprising that Wally was the first and last of that generation to enjoy a grammar school education. Mum was proud of his success. She cried when, near the end of her life, she told me that on one occasion some pupils in Plymouth had jeered at him because of the patches and darns in his school uniform, lovingly and carefully mended by their mother.

Mum made the most of the schooling that she received. Mrs Bettes had given her a few piano lessons when she was at Bridge School, and now she started to take regular lessons with Mr Leonard Ash at Geasons.

'Mr Ash made me blush when he called me out to the front to play a piece to the class.'

A little later, Mum began to take piano lessons with Miss Chubb in the dark drawing-room of her house, hidden behind a dense laurel hedge, in the terrace where Mr and Mrs Baple lived. Miss Chubb used to smack her hand with a ruler if she made a mistake. It did not often happen. She encouraged Mum to go on to 'take theory', saying that she would become an excellent musician if she did so. Although there was no money for the extra lessons for that, Mum always played well, with feeling and accuracy. She won a music prize.

There was a good teacher of English at Geasons, Mrs Markham, and she encouraged her pupils to read some of the great works of English literature. Mum relished learning poetry. For all her shyness, she enjoyed reciting or performing it: Wordsworth's *Idle Shepherd Boys*, Tennyson's *The Brook* and *The Revenge*, and passages from Shakespeare's *The Merchant of Venice*, including Portia's speech in praise of mercy (her lifelong favourite). All the books that Mum read at school and in later years lived on in her heart and mind, stored there by her powerful memory, imprinting their lessons on her soul. Each term there were examinations in arithmetic, in reading and in the writing of compositions or essays.

Every week Mum used to go with Sam, her family's spaniel, to take the rent to Mrs Damerell, the farmer's wife who owned the house. Mrs Damerell told Mum how much she admired Mrs Jarrold for keeping the house so clean and looking so neat and tidy, with the ten of them living there. But now Mum's family had to move. In the economic confusion that followed the Great War Mrs Damerell had to sell the house to raise money to enable her husband, who was much older than herself, to save the farm.

In late 1922, eight months before Mum left school, the family moved to a small council estate of red-brick houses, newly built for soldiers returning from the Great War – 'homes fit for heroes' as they were known – a little to the northwest, on the far side of the valley and the railway line. Their house, number 7 Stone Barton, would stay in the family for more than sixty years. To celebrate their move and to mark her thirteenth birthday, Mum planted a lilac tree beside the front door.

At about the same time Henry suffered a serious heart attack, and he had to retire. Dr Stamp told Agnes that her husband had not many months to live. His heart trouble often made his sallow, square face and his bald head flush, and become red. Agnes was determined to keep Henry alive and well and gave him a healthy diet with no red meat, fat or cream, Mum told me.

Plympton's population rose to about five thousand by the mid-1920s. The village remained peaceful and little changed.

'We had simple treats. I remember Mother and her sister, Aunt Emily, taking us in a donkey cart to Wembury to see the sea. Sometimes Jakey the donkey would not move, and Mother stood in front encouraging him with carrots.'

At home, Mum was still treated as the baby of the family. 'I was still playing with dolls when I was thirteen years old,' she told me. She was amused and a little ashamed that she had been so slow to grow up.

※

A friendly community grew up at Stone Barton. Each house was home to a family big by today's standards. It was a world, and a class, without the scars of divorce. Gardens were gardens, not yards concreted over for cars. Children could play safely outside all day. They grew up together, forging links that were to last eighty years in some cases. This was so for Mum. It gave her great joy.

Mum's parents were pillars of this society, the sort of people to whom others turned for comfort and help. Perhaps this was because of their experience, wider than that of many of the locals; perhaps it was because they were older than many of the other heads of households; but almost certainly their character, especially Agnes', is an important part of the explanation.

Henry was 5'9" tall, of stocky build and had a sallow complexion. His bearing was erect and he carried himself well, impressive as a butler, receiving obedience from all the servants below stairs. He was a smart man who always dressed formally, with a collar and tie, and had a serious and sometimes solemn face. He could be stern. His voice was deep, with a Midlands accent, and he used it dramatically. He ruled the family firmly. Even at the end, when he was often in bed because of heart tremors, he directed the family's life decisively. Everything he did was tinged with a certain sense of theatre. 'I'm going,' he would say if he felt a palpitation and all the family would gather around his bed.

For all this, Henry was loved by his family and respected with affection by the neighbours. He was a benign version of his cruel father, perhaps civilised and redeemed by his exceptional wife.

Agnes was a little taller than her husband. She was an imposing person, with a presence. Everyone spoke of 'Mrs Jarrold' in a respectful tone of voice that seemed to acknowledge special qualities. As long as there were people in Plympton who remembered her, for fifty years after her death, this tone of voice could be heard when people spoke of her.

Agnes' own voice was resonant, with a Midlands accent. Her face was oval and rather thin, with a pale complexion and dark grey eyes. The expression on her face was peaceful and calm, and often serious. Her straight hair, now white, she wore in a bun. She had an erect, Victorian posture. Her walk remained brisk until her last years. Then she began to slow down and to hobble a little, but she never made use of a stick.

Agnes was simple in her tastes and manner, and rather austere except on special occasions. When she was making mince-pies at Christmas, singing hymns and carols, she sipped from a glass of stout set on the corner of the kitchen range. Above all, she was kind and considerate. The only thing that mattered to her was the well-being of the family.

Agnes was a beloved matriarch, in charge of the day-to-day running of the house. She, rather than Henry, was the brains of their long and successful partnership. 'She was endowed with a great capacity for loving people. She was marvelous. She gave everything to them,' my cousin John told me.

And Mum told me: 'Father was always smartly dressed and always raised his hat to a lady. "Without manners, there is nothing," he used to say. He was very steadfast, stern and caring, a good man. My mother used to say how strong he was. Mother used to recite a poem to me:

> It's easy enough to be pleasant
> When life flows along like a song,
> But the one worthwhile
> Is the one who can smile
> When everything goes dead wrong.
> The test of the heart is trouble,
> And it always comes with the years;
> But the one who is worth
> The salt of the earth
> Is the one who can smile through tears.'

※

One August Bank Holiday when Mum was in her seventies, Judy and I sat with her under Dad's pear tree in her little back-garden. We listened to *Dear Octopus* by Dodie Smith, one of Mum's favourite plays. It is the story of a family, 'that dear octopus', under pressure in various ways, but somehow managing to hold together. The play ends with a speech delivered by the father of the clan at a family party.

As Mum wrote of another of her favourite plays, 'It is family life as it really was a few years ago, people really standing up for each other.'

12
'When you and I were seventeen'

MUM LEFT SCHOOL in July 1923 with a good report, as well as with her prizes.

'I left school a few months before I was fourteen. I had won a prize for my work. Mrs Birdwood presented me with it, a book called *The Flower of the Family*. She said to me, 'I hope that you will be the flower of your family.'

Mr Baple wrote in Mum's report, 'I cannot praise her too highly as a gifted and dutiful pupil.'

Her mother and father assured her that Mr Baple had, indeed, given her a wonderful report to mark the end of her school days.

※

In the autumn Mum started work just before her fourteenth birthday. There was little choice of jobs. Years later she told me, 'If I had my time again, knowing what I know now, I would have gone on with botany.' She loved to search for flowers and plants in the fields, woods and hedges and identify rare finds in the well-thumbed books handed on by her parents.

At another time she pondered a different possibility. It was when she was travelling to Moorhaven Hospital three times a week to visit Dad. She got to know the Matron of one of the Plymouth hospitals who said that she would be pleased to offer Mum a job. 'The nurses are so kind and thoughtful to all the patients, and, if I had my time again, I would try to be a nurse. They are so wonderful.'

Mum's two sisters were by now well into their twenties. Like their parents before them they had gone 'into service'. There were twenty or so substantial country houses in the rich farming country around Plympton offering such work, and Edie and Hilda 'lived in' as maids. Things were beginning to change even then in the early 1920s. Because of the slump in farming, the landed families were cutting back on servants. Perhaps Mum's mother felt that her youngest was too young for her years and too home-loving to move out and live with other servants in a country house and work for a strange family.

Whatever the reason, Mum took a different route. In August 1923 she began to work at Northcott's, a small drapery shop in Ridgeway. She received 3s 9d (19p) a week. She gave her mother three shillings; the nine pence that she kept, she spent on a bun or a slice of Russian cake and a glass of milk at Mr Heathman's dairy, or liquorice at Mrs Gent's sweetshop.

Mum enjoyed her work at Northcott's. She became fond of the elderly spinster who ran the shop. She observed her fussy manners and took in her droll words about her customers. She stored it all away.

Mum always loved Ridgeway, and that love went back to her childhood. 'I was happy with life as it was. If we wanted a treat, we just went to Ridgeway. You wouldn't believe that would you? And it was so nice when the Christmas tree was set up there and covered with lights.'

The confirmation service at St Mary's church was a big event each year, especially for the school-leavers.

In November 1924, when she was fifteen, Mum was one of the thirty-nine parishioners confirmed at St Mary's. The Bishop who conducted the service preached on a text from the Book of Revelation, 'Be faithful unto death,' words inscribed on the flyleaf of the small prayer book presented to each of the candidates.

Until about 1960 around half of the local school-leavers were confirmed each year in Plympton, between forty and sixty of them. Several adults would also be confirmed. In those fifteen years after the Second World War the ways and manner of life in the village were more like those of the 1920s and 1930s than what followed.

※

After working at Northcott's for a few months Mum moved to a more promising job at Yeo's department store in Plymouth. Her mother had taken her to Plymouth to buy an apprenticeship at one of the stores in the city. The first shop that they visited was Dingles, 'But I wasn't smart enough for Dingles,' Mum said, 'so we settled on Yeo's.'

The choice of Yeo's turned out well for Mum and she made the most of her opportunity. She made some friendships which lasted a lifetime. The apprenticeship gave her training in each department in turn. She loved the shop and the daily routine. Each morning she travelled from Plympton station on the 8.40 train to North Road station. 'There were a lot of smart girls on the train. One worked at Pophams.' Normally she took the short walk from the station to Yeo's, although from time to time she caught a tram.

At midday, when the weather was fine, she used to buy a sandwich or pasty. With her friends, she would walk up to The Hoe and they would eat their lunch looking out over the waters of Plymouth Sound.

Mum still felt very young for her years: 'I was a thin little girl standing behind the counter – very skinny.

'At first I used to earn ten shillings [50p] a week. I used to give the brown envelope to Mother: she had a lovely way of receiving and giving. Then, at the end of the apprenticeship, my wages went up to £1 a week. To celebrate this increase Mother bought me a grey flannel suit with a waistcoat, and a Scottish 'shanter with a tassel, at a shop in Old Town Street. I felt lovely in that outfit.'

Mum became popular at Yeo's. The owner, Major Frank Yeo, 6' 4" tall and distinguished in bearing, used to tease her. 'You have grown a lot since I last saw you', he said when he told her of her increase to £1 a week. Mum's height of 5' 10" made her noticeable in those days when most young women were so much shorter than they are now. The manager, John Beckley, also used to pull her leg. 'You are fit only for the carpet department', he said and she pretended to be furious.

On Wednesdays, when the shops closed for a half-day, Mum sometimes went to the pictures with a friend. Saturday was a full working day.

The other girls working at Yeo's were interested in Mum's big family. 'How many brothers have you got, Jarrold?' they asked her. (The girls used each others' surnames at work.) When she replied, 'Five,' they asked, 'Can we come out to Plympton and see you next Wednesday afternoon?'

Once a week, after work, her mother used to go into Plymouth on the 5.09 train. Mum would treat her to tea at Goodbody Matthews' café in George Street, near St Andrew's Cross. Mum would feel so proud of her when one of the girls called out, 'Your mother has arrived, Jarrold.'

They would drink a pot of tea or small cups of strong coffee with cream, and eat tiny, delicate sandwiches and delicious cakes which they used to share, half each, so that each of them tasted everything. A string trio, made up of tall, thin ladies with reading-glasses and long noses would play light classical and salon music, such as Kreisler's *Caprice Viennoise*, Paderewski's *Minuet in G* and *Chanson du Voyageur*, or Elgar's *Chanson de Matin*. There was a certain homeliness, but with a hint of romance, even elegance, in the busy, thriving city.

The two of them would then go to the pictures. They often saw dramatisations of classic novels, *Wuthering Heights*, *The Hunchback of Notre Dame*, and *Anna Karenina*. *The Barretts of Wimpole Street* was a favourite. They used to catch the 9.20 train back to Plympton station.

Mum's father worried about her. One day, when she was seventeen and was dressed up 'to go out flirting, Dad took me aside. I was wearing a black coat with an astrakhan collar and a French cloche hat. Dad told me "that I looked like a "Piccadilly Pat". Dad was stern in my flirting days.'

'I was a perfect nuisance when I was seventeen,' Mum told me. 'I used to keep Mum and Dad up late, till eleven o'clock, when I was out flirting. I fell for the curate at St Mary's, but I didn't dare to speak to him. I was seventeen and he was forty...'

Mr Brooks used to cut my hair with a fringe, or a shingle, or an Eton crop, at his shop in Ridgeway.

※

One day nearly seventy years later, Joan Vincent, one of Mum's oldest friends from Stone Barton, visited her in Ward 12. They talked about the old days. Together they sang one of the songs from a pantomime that they had seen at the Palace Theatre so long ago:

> When you and I were seventeen,
> And love and life were new,
> The world was just a field of green,
> With smiling skies of blue,
> That lovely spring when you were King
> And I was then your Queen;
> Can you recall when love was all,
> And we were seventeen?[3]

---

3 I have kept Mum's words even when they differ slightly from the original text of songs or poems, an indication of how her memory stood up to the passing of many years.

13
'Tea at Gunters'

ALTHOUGH MUM WAS, in her words, 'timid and anxious' when she started work in 1924, she had already begun to spread her wings. With one of her school friends, Millie Hayes, she went with two young men, riding pillion on a motorcycle, to the seaside for the day. 'I was nearly blown away by the wind, and then got cold swimming there.'

In late 1926 or early 1927, she and Wally visited their relations in London. It was the first time that she had stayed away from her home. Perhaps their parents arranged for them to go there for a holiday to help Wally put the traumatic events of the General Strike behind him.

Wally had reached his sixteenth birthday and left the Grammar School in the summer of 1922. He passed his school certificate with flying colours and received 'matriculation exemption' for university, but there was no question of his taking that up. With his mother he visited various offices in Plymouth and she helped him get a job. He joined the Great Western Railway and started work as a booking-clerk.

'Wal was nervous and mother gave him confidence,' Mum told me.

Wally spent all his working life on the railways, first the G.W.R. and later British Railways. He was not at all well paid at first. In his family only he and perhaps, in those days, Jack held strong political views. In a small way Wally became involved in the turmoil of the General Strike in May 1926. Perhaps Jack influenced him.

Railway men, dockers, and bus drivers went on strike in support of the coal miners, who had rejected a cut in their wages and had been locked out of the mines by the pit owners.[4] Wally joined in. The strike began to collapse after a few days. On the twelfth of May the Trade Union Congress backed down and called it off. The miners remained on strike until mid-November, when they could do nothing but accept the wage cuts, the prospect of which had provoked the strike in the first place.

The end of the strike was of international significance. In Moscow Trotsky, Lenin's closest associate in the Bolshevik seizure of power in October 1917, regarded the strike's failure as decisive in forestalling Communist advances in Europe. After the fall of the Soviet Union in 1991 Kremlin papers revealed that the Soviet Communist Party had secretly sent funds to their allies among the British strikers, a fact which was wholly unknown by, and would undoubtedly have been repugnant to, the bulk of those on strike, like Wally.

Wally was sacked. His dismissal was a terrible blow for him, so young and at the beginning of his career,

---

[4] In 1925 the government made the terrible mistake of returning the pound sterling to the gold standard at the parity in force until 1914. This made British goods too dear to win or to keep markets overseas, and caused unemployment. Wages were cut to balance companies' books. The General Strike was the direct result of the government's grievous error.

and for his parents. They had staked so much on his education and were distraught. His mother put on her smart black dress, hat and coat, and went to Flete House to call on Lord Mildmay. He was a director of the company, and he agreed to take Wally back onto the payroll.

Mum told me that his actions in the strike had deeply upset their mother: 'She wasn't going to let Wally down, but it wasn't easy for her to bow the knee and she came home and cried, although she had succeeded.'

Wally grieved that his mother had had to do this for him. He believed that he had played a part in humiliating her. His political views greatly moderated as the years passed. He never spoke of what had happened in 1926.

※

So for two weeks Mum and Wally stayed with their Uncle Jack, their mother's brother, and his wife, Auntie Nellie. Uncle Jack and Auntie Nellie lived in a flat on the third floor of Balderton Buildings, a Peabody Trust property in Brown Hart Gardens near Oxford Street. Jack was now the mainstay of the Aldersey family, eight brothers and sisters whom he worked hard to keep in touch with one other.

It took Mum a while to overcome her homesickness. 'Will she ever stop crying?' Uncle Jack demanded. 'She'll have to go home if she doesn't stop "whinnicking". I can't bear it any longer.'

Mum stopped. She was enjoying the thrill of being in the capital of the greatest empire the world had ever seen. It was too much to risk being sent home early. Besides, Auntie Nellie was a wonderful cook.

Uncle Jack had gone into service as a young man as a valet and butler. By 1927 he had been working for some time at Gunters, the well-known Mayfair tearoom in Curzon Street. He welcomed the customers and assisted them with their hats and coats. Knowing him well, they gave him generous tips. He had a distinguished, courteous manner and a gallant bearing. To her pride, Uncle Jack introduced Mum to his regular customers as 'my niece, up from the country'. The staff there regarded him as their father or elder brother. He and Nellie could have no children of their own.

At the end of each day Uncle Jack used to take home a few tiny sandwiches and exquisite cakes that had been left over. Mum's memories of these treats caused her to dream of that visit to London whenever Gunters was mentioned. In her seventies, by when the teashop had long since ceased to exist, she relished a play on the radio, *Tea at Gunters*.

Mum and Wally explored London. They ventured onto the Serpentine in Hyde Park in a rowing-boat. Wally was infuriated when Mum could not give him clear directions as he rowed; she circled in one spot or zigzagged across the lake. But Wally was proud of his sister. With her good looks and smart clothes, a new suit with a hat and shoes bought specially for the visit, she made a good impression on everyone that they met. 'You're the best-looking girl in London,' he said to her.

At the end of their holiday they went shopping in Oxford Street and the Edgware Road. They bought seven parcels, presents for their aunt and uncle, and others to take back to Plympton. As they went back to the flat, exhausted from walking the length of Edgware Road, Mum noticed that one of her parcels was missing. She had twisted the string of each one around one of her fingers and somehow had dropped one.

Wally was furious. The missing present was a pair of red slippers for Auntie Nellie. They retraced their steps and bought another pair. They made their way back to Balderton Buildings for their last evening together. Auntie Nellie gave Mum a gold bangle bracelet. A few years later, when her mother's eyesight grew weak, Mum sold it and used the money to buy her a hymn-book with large print, which her mother used every Sunday. Uncle Jack gave Mum a smart top-coat, made by his tailor.

The next day Uncle Jack and Auntie Nellie saw Wally and Mum off at Paddington station. Mum had become their favourite niece.

※

In the 1970s, fifty years after that fortnight in London, Judy and I took Mum to Brown Hart Gardens. Auntie Nellie, and after her Uncle Jack, had died long ago. Auntie Alice, Jack's second wife, was still living there as her life in its turn was drawing to its end.

It was the August bank holiday. In the 'Seventies most of the shops in Oxford Street used to close for the holiday. The centre of London was deserted and quiet. We found plenty of parking space for our car, not far from the Ukrainian Uniate cathedral, and walked to Balderton Flats, as the block had been renamed. We met no one on the way there. It was as if, for a moment, we were in the past, and Wally and Mum, still young people of twenty and seventeen years, might come around the corner, on their way back from the Serpentine or from their shopping adventure in the Edgware Road, with their parcels.

Auntie Alice was a rather frail lady by this time, slight in build, with a pale, round face, glasses, and a pointed nose. She was cheerful and bright, and kept the flat beautifully clean and tidy, with many mementoes of Uncle Jack, and of Auntie Nellie's days. Auntie Alice was as fond of Mum as had been Auntie Nellie. She gave us a wonderful plum tart for tea. We washed up together in her little kitchen. Auntie Alice and Mum reminisced about Uncle Jack and the Aldersey family, and Auntie Alice was interested in us and our doings.

Over the next couple of years Judy and I took Mum to visit her twice more, the last time not long before Auntie Alice's final illness. Mum told me that her niece had written to tell her, 'She is quite happy but living in a little world of her own.'

Auntie Alice died in the early spring of 1980. In her will she left Mum £500. Mum was overwhelmed by this generous and kind act, the only occasion when she received any money in a will, except for £8 from her mother, and, of course, everything that Dad had left. 'I have not got used to it yet,' she told me. 'I never wanted to receive money through anyone dying. It was good that you took me to see her.'

Mum used the money to renew the electrical wiring in her house, just in time for Christmas that year.

※

After returning with Wally to Devon from London, Mum went back to work at Yeo's. She was enjoying her time there. She loved dealing with customers and selling hats and flowers, shirts and hosiery. She was unhappy for a while in the despatch department. One of the staff there was dishonest and tried to lead her astray. Mum had to stand up to her.

Apart from that short time, the atmosphere was cheerful and kind and full of jokes. When it was time for the customers to leave and for the doors to be locked at the end of the day, one of the managers used to go quickly from floor to floor, calling out, 'Have you cleared your drawers, girls?'

Mum worked at Yeo's for seven happy years until 1931.

By then, all unknown to her for many more years, Dad had been in India for a decade.

※

Mum's life in the late 1920s and early 1930s revolved around home and work, her family and her colleagues. She continued to read quite widely.

The family went on a few special outings. When Castle Drogo, near Drewsteignton, was given to the National Trust by the Drewe family in 1974, Mum told me, 'I saw it when I was about eighteen, out for a drive with my Mum and Dad in a taxi we hired for an outing. I thought it was lovely and the scenery superb.'

At school Mum had made a good friend, Marietta Burgess. Marietta was a lively girl, with a turned-up nose. She loved to visit Mum's house, and used to sit on the kitchen table, with her feet on a chair, playing her ukulele. 'Mother loved her because she made her laugh,' Mum told me.

The Burgesses lived in a detached house at the end of Stone Barton, opposite Treverbyn, the grand offices of the Rural District Council. Plympton St Mary was believed to be the most extensive Rural District in England at that time. The red-brick building, with its fine granite gateway, was demolished in the 1990s.

Mr Burgess was a senior officer in the R.D.C. His steady rise at work – eventually he became Clerk to the Council – put him in a small, professional class in Plympton, unlike the fathers of Mum's other friends.

The Burgesses used to take Mum along on outings in their Morris Cowley as company for Marietta. Wearing hats with wide brims and veils to protect their hair, the two girls used to sit in the open dicky seat, with the hood down. The Burgesses had a family link with North Devon and once in summer they took Mum to Combe Martin. They gave her many good outings.

Marietta became a pretty young woman.

'I was jealous of her when she got a boyfriend,' Mum said. 'She was soon engaged to be married and made a good match. I gave her a wedding present, and she was a lovely bride, but she didn't invite me to the wedding.

'When Mr Burgess came in to see Mother in the kitchen afterwards I was there. He must have realised that I was a bit sad and disappointed.

'"I hoped you wouldn't feel like that, Grace," he said. "You know what they are like. It's all gloss and veneer."

'Mr Burgess was ashamed of the way they treated me.'

Marietta's turned-up nose proved to be symbolic. She had inherited, or adapted her ways to, her mother's snobbery. Mr Burgess' success did not change him. He continued to visit the kitchen at number 7, and to give Mum some of the strawberries that he grew in his back garden, which she loved. She admired the way in which he established primroses and meadowsweet in the hedge in front of his house.

※

One afternoon, more than sixty years later, I am sitting beside Mum's bed in Ward 12. It is the quiet period when the nurses and helpers have collected all the plates and cutlery. Some of the patients have nodded off. I have just given Mum some early Cornish strawberries. Perhaps they remind her of her happy memories of the times when Mr Burgess brought her family some of his.

'He was a nice man,' she says. But her mind moves on to the story of Marietta's wedding, and she reminds me of it.

After a long pause, she adds, 'I was no worse than Marietta.'

Mum absorbed the pain of that 'bit of snobbery' and rejection into herself. She could not imagine that she would reject anyone for such a reason. She had thought, at the time, that what had happened must show that Marietta and her mother felt that there was something inferior about her in a deeper way.

Something entered Mum's heart (perhaps it was always there) that made her feel unworthy, unaccepted and, for some reason she could not fathom, unacceptable. Only now, at the end of her life, does Mum come to realise and say openly that she does not believe that any longer. 'Marietta felt that they were a step higher than us. It was sad, really. I was a bit hurt. I felt as good as anybody. I was always proud of mother. I thought she was wonderful.

'A lot of us are nobodies and go through the world feeling that, and getting no recognition. Some people are noticed all the time and they don't realise that other people are sad because they are unappreciated and unnoticed. In a way, it's bad to be noticed too much, because then you expect it all the time, and it's painful if it doesn't arrive. There's a great gap there, and others don't know what you're missing...

'I mustn't snivel. When life is at its healthiest, make the most of it. Don't take it for granted. Mother used to say 'Life is a burden – bear it. Life is a crown of thorns – wear it.' It's hard, but most of it is lovely. Don't be frightened... There is always someone to pick up the pieces; it's strange but there always is.'

14

'The test of the heart is trouble'

IN OCTOBER 1930 Mum's family held a party for her twenty-first birthday. Her parents gave her a gold wristwatch.

Not long after that, in the early 'Thirties, Mum gave up her job at Yeo's. She always regretted doing so. She had been doing well and enjoyed the work.

'I should have done what I wanted, but one of the other girls kept saying that she hated the work, and she influenced me. Mother wanted me to stay at Yeo's.'

So, in her early twenties, Mum settled into a life of helping her mother to keep house for her father and her four unmarried brothers. Both her sisters and one of her brothers were already married. By now her mother really needed her help.

After bearing eight children Agnes had suffered a miscarriage. For twenty-five years she had moved with Henry and their growing family from house to house around the country wherever his work had taken him. She had lived through the Great War of 1914 to 1918, constantly fearing for her two eldest sons, in the Royal Artillery and the Cavalry. She had lived solely for her family, to make them happy. She had succeeded, and, at the age of sixty four, she was exhausted.

Henry had been a semi-invalid for several years. For a while, at the start of the Great War, he worked in the Royal Naval dockyard at Devonport. He was by then in his late forties, and his health broke down. 'You can't make a race-horse do the work of a cart-horse, Mrs Jarrold,' Dr Stamp told Agnes when he visited them at number 7 in his pony and trap, wearing his formal suit and top-hat.

Henry was able to go back to work as a butler after a time but he suffered a heart attack in 1923, when he was fifty-five years old.

One sunny day in the early spring of that year during the Easter holidays he had walked home from work at Tamerton through Plymbridge woods, which had been white with snowdrops a few weeks earlier. Agnes and Mum were in the midst of washing up the midday dinner dishes. Mum was thirteen at the time. She was in her last year at school.

Soon after he arrived home Henry collapsed over the kitchen table. With Mum's help, Agnes made a fire for Henry in their bedroom and they settled him there. Dr Stamp told Agnes that Henry might die at any moment and, in any case, had not many months to live. 'We'll see about that,' Agnes said.

Henry's health improved gradually. Although he had to retire, he quite soon re-asserted himself as head of the household. 'Mother treated him like gold dust,' Mum told me.

Henry had enjoyed his work as a butler. The years of enforced retirement were not easy for him or Agnes.

In earlier years they had taken their children to the pantomime each Christmas at the Palace Theatre in Plymouth. One year there was a song which Agnes and Mum used to sing to make light of the unstinting care that they now had to give Henry:

> I wake him in the morning when the clock
>   strikes eight;
> I'm always punctual, never, never late:
> A nice cup of tea and a little round of toast,
> *The Sporting Life* and *The Winning Post*.
> I make him nice and comfy
> Then I toddle off to work –
> For I'm only doing what a woman should do,
> For he's only a working man.

Each morning Mum took her father tea in bed, followed a little later by his shaving water in a gunmetal mug and a bowl of water to be put on his wash-stand. Henry got up and vigorously splashed himself with a flannel. He spent the rest of the morning resting upstairs in the bedroom, with its peaceful green and cream wallpaper, decorated with rose patterns.

In the afternoon he took his 'constitutional' in the lanes around Plympton, leaning on his walking stick with its silver handle.

This peaceful routine gave him another sixteen years' life.

※

'In the morning I would clean the house and go to the shops at Colebrook', Mum told me. 'In the afternoon I would sometimes go for a ride on my Raleigh bike to Lee Moor and free-wheel back down the lanes from the edge of Dartmoor. Then I would cut dozens of thin slices of bread and butter for tea. The seven of us would sit down around the dining-table together, with a huge plate of bread and butter at each end of the table, and one of Mother's rabbit pies if we were lucky.'

Once a week in the 'Thirties Mum and her mother continued to go to Plymouth on the 5.09 pm train for tea at Goodbody Matthews, and a film at the Gaumont or Andrews cinema. They would return on the 9.20 train. It was the highlight of their week.

On Sundays they would go to the service at St Mary's church. They also listened to services on the radio.

※

Perhaps Agnes and Henry made their home too happy and their children too welcome. Most of them were rather slow to get married and to begin their own families.

'We were always jolly in our house. Mother always had her hands in flour, cooking for us hungry ones... We always seemed to have a nice meal put before us. My mother knew the way to cook a meal. My brothers went rabbiting, and no one could roast rabbits like Mother. She made bread and saffron cake in the Cornish range. We all loved saffron cake.'

Harry, the eldest son, married Maggie in February 1920. He was twenty-four years old and his work on the G.W.R. took him from time to time to her home town in South Wales.

Edie was the next to marry. She was twenty-four when she settled down with her husband, Len, in April 1921. Len was also a railwayman.

Jack, three years younger than Edie, never married. He had been fifteen years old when the Great War broke out, and had joined the Army a year or two later to serve in the Cavalry. The experience affected him more deeply than Harry.

'Jack was a very gentle man,' Mum said. 'Quite the opposite of warlike... It must have been awful for him to kill people who had never done him a bit of harm...'

In war and peace Jack found comfort when he went for long walks in the woods at dawn or dusk with his many dogs. He did jobbing gardening to earn his living, and enjoyed a quiet life at home. Late in his life he still used to go to the woods with his dogs in the early spring to listen to the dawn chorus.

'He was a very good man,' Mum said.

Hilda married Fred in July 1927. She was twenty-seven. Fred was well known in the village as a keen footballer and boxer.

George was two years younger than Hilda. He had a generous spirit, quick wits and good looks. He did not marry.

※

For eight years after Hilda's wedding in 1927 Mum lived at number 7 with her parents, Jack, George and her two youngest brothers Arthur and Wally. From 1931 she was at home, full-time, helping her mother keep house for the five men-folk.

The pattern of life at number 7 was broken in the mid-1930s when, within a year of each other, Wally and Arthur moved away.

Wally was doing well on the railway. Like others in the family, he found in it a responsible and worthwhile job. In October 1935, less than ten years after the General Strike that had caused him such trouble, he and Audrey married, with Arthur as Wally's best man. Wally and Audrey set up home in a newly-built house on the far side of Plymouth, about six miles away from number 7, not far from the River Tamar and the Royal Navy's dockyard at Devonport.

In the summer of 1936 it was Wally's turn to act as Arthur's best man when he married Edna in June 1936.

'Arthur was a "belonger", like me. He used to go to eight o'clock Holy Communion and evensong at St Mary's. We all loved him. How much he used to help us all.

'Arthur and Edna eventually had five flower, fruit and vegetable shops in Plymouth. They were all bombed out in the Blitz.'

Arthur and Edna's marriage was tragically short.

As a boy, Arthur had hurt himself badly in an accident when he and his brothers were playing at the railway station. He slipped down between the platform and a stationary train. The fall bruised his back. Wishing not to worry his parents he did not tell them about it. Not long after his marriage, this wound reappeared and it became infected with tuberculosis. It ended a happy marriage and killed a generous, loving man.

The loss of her dearest brother, on Boxing Day 1938, coming so early in his promising life, haunted Mum for the rest of her days. He was only thirty-four years old.

Of the eight children in the family, Arthur and Mum were the two most alike in character and, in affection, the closest to each other. Arthur had constantly sustained Mum with his moral support. He was a happy, kind man, full of fun, steady and always thoughtful. He had a buoyant, jolly outlook, and an infectious guffaw of a laugh.

Edna remarried during the Second World War. For the rest of her life, she arranged for flowers to be placed on Arthur's grave at Christmas. Even after her death in 1979 there would be a wreath delivered on the instructions that Edna made in her will. The sight of the flowers there each year, in frosty sunshine or in Devon mist, always touched Mum's heart and caused her to shed some tears as she stood in silence at his grave, not far from where Arthur and Edna had lived together for such a short time.

※

One day in Ward 12, stirring herself from deep thought, Mum smiled and said to me: 'I was afraid that I'd forgotten Arthur's face, but I haven't.

'People came all the way from the Channel Islands for his funeral, because of all the flowers grown there that he and Edna had sold.

'It's because he died so young and you never know what is going to happen to anyone that I am so keen on people being nice to each other. You never know what you are doing to people...

'Arthur was sensible and saved money. He was generous to people in need. He didn't tell anyone about it, and we found out after his death. Miss Mewton who lived in a tiny house in Ridgeway didn't have much money. She was a lovely lady and she told us that Arthur had given her five shillings. He bought Mother and Father a lovely suite of furniture for number 7...'

After a pause, Mum added: 'It's been a lovely life, a very good life... I didn't much like being thirty, but everything was fine later.'

And only now does the penny drop for me that it was of this period, just after Wally had married Audrey, and Arthur had married Edna, that Mum spoke least often. In the years until 1938, she had been able to look forward to Arthur's daily visits to number 7.

Every day, after working at their shop nearby in Colebrook, on his way home to Edna at Hooe, he would call on his family. Often he took them a small treat, a quarter of clotted cream or some flowers or fruit. To the end of her life Mum's eyes would light up when she told me of these visits.

With his death, everything changed. Mum lost much of the warmth and cosiness that she craved all her life. She was twenty-nine.

※

Henry died in late October 1939, his death hastened by the anxiety that he felt because of the second German war in his lifetime.

Towards the end of that month's Indian summer, Henry arrived home one day for tea after an unusually long walk. He had gone to visit the last big house where he had served as butler, at Tamerton Foliot.

At the gate he congratulated Jack and George on the progress they were making with the air-raid shelter in the front garden.

Mum greeted him at the front door, as usual. She had already cut the bread and spread it with margarine for his tea. The kettle was bubbling on the range. The teapot was warming. As Mum took her father's Homburg hat and walking stick from him, he fell dead in her arms. It was the eve of her thirtieth birthday.

Agnes lived on for nearly four years.

One night in July 1943 during the renewed blitz of Plymouth, she decided to sit outside in the garden and watch the flames rising high into the sky from the horrifying fires as the bombs fell on the city. The heat in the stuffy shelter had made her feel unwell, and she did not want to stay there for the whole of the alert. Well into the night she was hit by the blast from a bomb dropped by a German bomber as it sped eastwards, making its getaway from the anti-aircraft defences that surrounded Plymouth.

Agnes took to her bed and died a few days later, surrounded by her children.

Mum went wild with grief. For more than ten years she had been caring for elderly parents and two curmudgeonly brothers, with little joy, help or encouragement. First Arthur's death, then those of her parents, the unending pressure of the war and the thankless drudgery of looking after Jack and George, knocked Mum off balance. The prospects looked bleak. She was thirty-three years old and most of the eligible men were married or away in the Services at the War. She had never lacked admirers, and she soon found herself briefly engaged to Les, a family friend from the Midlands.

One afternoon early in August, Grace gave way to her grief for her mother. She mixed together half a bottle of gin and brandy in a strong cocktail, and began to play the piano. She very rarely drank alcohol, and the effect was extreme. In the little back drawing-room, she told me, the piano began to sway to and fro under the powerful attack of her normally lyrical, sensitive fingers. Various members of the family gathered in the hallway and peered around the door from time to time. Finally, someone led her upstairs to recover in her bedroom, at the front of the house. From her window she caught sight of Les and called out to him, 'Go to hell, you bugger!'

Mum was no fool. For all her simplicity of soul and singleness of heart, she did not miss much. People underestimated her intelligence, or her insight into the devices and desires of those around her, at their peril.

As it turned out, the word that Mum used was apt but completely uncharacteristic of her. Les was later discovered to be the boy-friend of her cousin George, a married man who lived with his family in Nottingham.

The next day, chastened and overwhelmed by guilt, Grace returned the engagement ring to Les, who primly told her to wash her mouth out with disinfectant and to go to church to pray for forgiveness. Without a doubt, she did the latter. She 'signed the pledge' and on that day became teetotal. Apart from the brandy on the plum pudding at Christmas, and in her last years an occasional spoonful of it when she felt, in her word, 'squawmish', she kept her pledge.

That action was not enough, on its own, to restore Mum's equilibrium.

She was courted by Charles Smith, a naval officer, who gave her an unofficial engagement ring. He also gave her some romantic piano music – Liszt's *Liebes-*

traum number 3 and *A Maiden's Prayer* by T. Badarzewska. Mum wrote on them, 'From Chas to Grace'.

It was around this time in 1944, not long after the humiliating nadir of Grace's fortunes, that Charlie Paul visited Dad at Saugor and spoke to him of her. Charlie had good reason to be confident of what he told Dad about Mum. As the shrewd witness who lived across the road from the Jarrolds' house in Stone Barton told me after Mum's death, 'I could see that there was something special about her. It was her integrity.'

※

On the fourth of December 1944 Mum met Dad. Everything changed.

15
Interlude

ON A QUIET SUMMER DAY in 1996, by when she had been in Ward 12 for eight months, Mum said to me, 'I'm looking forward to seeing Dad again... I didn't have long enough with Dad, only twenty-eight years.'

During the thirty-two months that she spent in hospital her thoughts often turned to him, memories happy and sad.

Once she told me, 'I thanked Dad for a lot of things a couple of days ago, more than ever before... He was a lovely husband and father... We had lovely times with Dad...

'He was too good for me, but he always thought that I was better than I was. Florrie shouldn't have made so much of me to Charlie...

'I'd love to hear Dad laugh now, to see him laugh... I loved his dry Cornish jokes... How much he loved you boys... Oxford University was his plan for you both... He was generous and gentle, always on the side of the loser, the one in need...

'He was the best thing that ever happened to me...

'Will you always think about Dad? I hope that he gets the reward that he deserves for being so lovely. He already has it, I think... Lovely Dad... God bless Dad from all of us. Thank you, Dad, for everything, for being so lovely to us. Thanks be to Dad, thanks be to God…

'I'm glad I had Jack for my husband… He was very clever to do what he did in life… Take care of his M.B.E., won't you? …

'Dad was lovely, wasn't he…?

'I was almost too happy with him…'

A month before Mum died, on the last visit when she could speak to me, I showed her a photo of Dad. I did that on so many visits. She recognised him immediately and her face came alive, 'I love that photo.'

And looking at the photo, she said to Dad, 'God bless you, my darling.'

16
Courtship and Marriage

IN THE EARLY 1990s Mum's independent days at home were drawing to an end. She had been a widow for twenty years, and she was determined to stay on as long as possible in the house where she and Dad had made their final home. They had lived there for most of their twenty seven and a half years together.

We did whatever practical things we could to help her, but it was more important, generally, to try to keep up her spirits and encourage her. One thing I did was to suggest that, on the long winter evenings when time hung heavy for her, she should write an account of some of her happy memories: 'Things that made us happy years ago,' I said. Mum took to the idea, a little reluctantly at first, and it used to improve her spirits.

As she sat by the coal fire in the sitting-room in the evening or at the kitchen table in the morning with her back to the comforting warmth of the Rayburn, converted from anthracite to oil soon after Dad's death, she put down on paper some of her thoughts and memories. She relived her happy days, and wrote them up in an old Basildon Bond writing pad.

One day she wrote:

> December 4th 1994 ... this is 50 years to the day since I first met Jack ... Next day we went by train from Plympton station to Totnes and then to Buckfastleigh. It was wonderful. We had a meal at the British Restaurant, of casserole and Manchester pudding. Then to a pub in Totnes where I treated him to a glass of beer. He was a really kind gentleman, and I think that we knew that we would marry.

At Buckfast Abbey a French monk was playing the violin, and the sound filled the peaceful building. There was no one else there.

In his pocket diary Dad kept a brief record of the events of those twelve busy days:

> Tuesday 5th. Took Grace to Buckfast Abbey and Totnes. A lovely day.
>
> Wednesday 6th. Took Grace to Shaugh [in the Plym valley]. Whitethorn [the pub where they had lunch]. Bed 2am.
>
> Thursday 7th. Went to Heybrook Bay with Grace – a lovely day.
>
> Friday 8th. Afternoon went to Meavy Church, Clearbrook with Grace. Skylark Inn.
>
> Saturday 9th. Saw Chaplain! [to arrange their wedding]. We went up to fix up rooms at Two Bridges but no luck. Arranged at Dartmeet.
>
> Sunday 10th. Church with Hilda and Wally am. Meavy with Grace pm. Bed 2.30am.
>
> Monday 11th. Left for Nora's. Very nice trip down.
>
> Tuesday 12th. Up to Clara's; and packed a box.
>
> Wednesday 13th. Left 9.30. Met Grace at North Road station. Lunch and then to Shaugh and Dewerstone.

Thursday 14th. Went to buy the rings at Page's in Plymouth but only took one. Had tea at Goodbody's. Did a lot of other shopping with Grace.

Friday 15th. Went with Grace and bought the engagement ring. Tea at Goodbody's, then to Plymbridge and walk home.

Saturday 16th. Married at 2pm in Plympton Church. We had a very nice party after the wedding. Left at 4.30pm for Dartmeet – Mrs James – a very quiet and beautiful house, and the country is thrilling.

And in her pale blue Basildon Bond pad Mum wrote:

December 16th 1994. This would be Dad's and my Golden Wedding. Fifty years ago at Stone Barton we prepared for our wedding at St. Mary's church. They carried up the carpet from Wal and Audrey's house on Plymouth Road, the stair carpet from Hilda and Fred's house [a little further along Stone Barton at number 84, on the other side of the road], and made number 7 look very smart.

The table was spread in the back room, and a great spread it was, although rationing was still on. Hilda got black-market food via Tom the policeman. The church was quite full. Jack [her brother] gave me away; Dad was very smart in his officer's uniform and me in a blue dress – very plain, but a buttonhole of red roses. The room was cram-full of family and neighbours. I played the piano, and John [Hilda's son] and Terry [Florrie's eldest son] sang and the rest of us joined in. Mr Scott – our next-door neighbour – said that it was the best wedding he had ever attended.

The taxi came, driven by Joan Littlejohns. The family and friends all made a long line on each side of the path to the gate. Jack and I went to get in the taxi, bound for Dartmeet, to the strains of *I'll Be with You in Apple Blossom Time*. It was pelting with rain. The next day it was just like summer and we went for a lovely walk on Dartmoor. Stayed there for two weeks. Then had a week in London! We went to several shows. Called to see Uncle Jack and Aunt Nellie at their flat.

It was sad when Jack's last day came, and he left the hotel to board the ship to travel back to India; me to return to Plympton.

On the last day of 1944 Mum wrote a message for Dad in his diary:

> We're at the Zoo – very nice. At the present moment we're contemplating roast beef very eagerly – frosty day and we're a trifle peckish. Been to Uncle Jack's yesterday and had a lovely supper. They like Jack, I can see. No wonder. He's such a dear.
>
> Now we've had hot bath and are ready for bed. It's New Year's Eve and London is like a mad place. Our last night together.
>
> After tomorrow is gone, may time fly until I see my lovely husband again. The world will be a very empty place when he's away from me. We are married, tho', and have the lovely future to look forward to.
>
> May God bless him and keep him safe until we meet again.

As Dad embraced Mum before leaving her, he quoted Shakespeare:

> Parting is such sweet sorrow
> That I shall say goodnight till it be morrow.

But Mum was not entirely alone as she returned to Plympton.

17
Home Thoughts from Abroad

AFTER DAD HAD SET OFF at the beginning of January 1945 on his return to India for the last time, Mum returned to Devon secretly carrying me within her.

Just after Germany's unconditional surrender to the Allies on the 7th of May, Charlie Paul wrote a letter to Dad. Charlie's unit was working to move troops and supplies eastwards into Burma in order to halt and reverse the Japanese invasion.

Charlie told Dad that he had heard from Florrie that Mum was finding it difficult now to summon up much enthusiasm for the thankless task of cooking and cleaning and caring for her brothers, Jack and George. Dad underlined some sentences in Charlie's letter and put an exclamation mark in the margin, drawn in the thick, Army-issue red pencil of the sort I remember from childhood, red at one end and blue at the other.

Apart from keeping house for Jack and George, Mum spent some weeks early in 1945 helping Wally and her sister-in-law Audrey, who had recently given birth to her second son.

Mum also found herself nursing back to health her Canadian cousin Ted, who had been a prisoner of war in Germany. Ted was the grandson of her mother's sister, who had emigrated from England to Canada after the First World War.

Like the other Dominions in the British Commonwealth, Australia, New Zealand and South Africa, Canada had declared war on Germany on the 3rd of September.

In 1940 Ted had bravely volunteered to come to England for service at a time when Canadians in their armed forces still had the right to choose to serve only in North America. Two years later, flying on a joint RAF/RCAF mission, he was shot down over France. Betrayed to the Germans by the French peasants who found him, he was taken to a prison camp in Germany, far to the east. He was held in the part of Germany that was given to Poland after the War when that country's eastern and western borders were moved two hundred miles to the west.

By 1945 Ted was emaciated. He was forced by his German guards to march west as they fled with their prisoners to escape the merciless horrors of the revenge exacted, on Stalin's orders, by the advancing Soviet Army. After his release by the British and a stay at the hospital for Canadian servicemen at Cliveden, he moved down to Devon to live for a while with Mum in Plympton. He was still only skin and bone, and the sight of him preyed on the mind of Florrie's fifteen-year-old son Jack.

Ted depended almost exclusively on Mum for his care during that time, recovering from what, as he later recalled, was an almost deranged state. He then went back to Canada and soon married Mary. Only in 1997, as his life neared its end, could he bring himself to revisit France.

Mum did not have an easy pregnancy. She had no one to care for her at number 7 during the three months after my birth; rather, she had to care for me in addition to her brothers. She had to work very hard, and developed varicose veins.

Throughout that difficult, listless year Dad wrote to her almost every day. When she set off for India to join him in January 1946, she left all these letters at number 7, safe in a box lined with pink satin, bequeathed to her by her mother. She had carefully tied them together in bundles with ribbons. On her return to England in the autumn of 1947, Mum was horrified to find that Jack and George had sold the inlaid box, and had thrown out Dad's letters and the other small treasures that her mother had left her in her informal will.

None of Dad's letters survives, but he used to copy out lines of poetry to send to Mum to soothe, comfort and encourage her. In his copy of Palgrave's Golden Treasury he annotated the verses that he sent her, with her name and the date when he wrote. This little blue volume, in the Oxford World Classics series, became precious to her, and in later years she often turned to it as a secure reminder of what she and Dad shared at that time, memories of their happiness.

After so long in India, twenty-three years by then, Dad's thoughts were becoming focused on settling down in England and the sort of home he and Mum might make. As the greatest heat of summer built up in the centre of the subcontinent, just before Midsummer Day, he copied out and sent to Mum some lines by Samuel Rogers (1763-1855):

A Wish

Mine be a cot beside the hill;
  A bee-hive's hum shall soothe my ear;
A willowy brook that turns a mill,
  With many a fall shall linger near.

The swallow, oft, beneath my thatch
  Shall twitter from her clay-built nest;
Oft shall the pilgrim lift the latch,
  And share my meal, a welcome guest.

Around my ivied porch shall spring
  Each fragrant flower that drinks the dew;
And Lucy, at her wheel, shall sing
  In russet gown and apron blue.

The village church among the trees,
  Where first our marriage vows were given,
With merry peels shall swell the breeze
  And point with taper spire to Heaven.

The 'cottage beside a hill' would become real within three years.

A few days later he sent Mum these lines by Robert Browning:

Home Thoughts from Abroad

Oh, to be in England now that April's there,
And whoever wakes in England sees, some morning, unaware,
That the lowest boughs and the brushwood sheaf
Round the elm tree bole are in tiny leaf,
While the chaffinch sings on the orchard bough
In England – now!

The last lines of the second stanza of these 'Home Thoughts' express how strongly Home must have been calling Dad:

> And though the fields look rough with hoary dew,
> All will be gay when noontide wakes anew
> The buttercups, the little children's dower
> – Far brighter than this gaudy melon flower!

For all his longing to go Home and settle down, Dad and his colleagues in India had a pressing sense of the size and urgency of what they had to do before they could relax. In his copy of the anthology *England*, compiled in 1944 by Harold Nicolson, Dad marked some lines in Rudyard Kipling's poem 'For All We Have and Are', written in 1914:

> There is but one task for all –
> One life for each to give.
> What stands if Freedom fall?
> Who dies if England live?

Many years after Dad's death, in the Family Bible that he had bought in May 1934, I found a sheet of paper to which he had pasted some flowers and leaves sent to him by Mum, with the following notes made by him:

> Wallflower
> Bluebell from Plymbridge
> Beech leaf
> Briar rose from Plymbridge.
> 3rd June 1945

Dad was full of hope. He had a strong faith that God ordered this world to our good, if only we cooperate with Him in His way. In July he sent Mum more lines by Browning. They came from *Pippa Passes*, the song that the innocent girl sang for the joy of life, despite her hardships and ragged clothes:

> The year's at the spring,
>   And day's at the morn;
>   Morning's at seven;
>   The hillside's dew-pearled;
>   The lark's on the wing;
>   The snail's on the thorn;
>   God's in his heaven –
>   All's right with the world!

Dad wrote some of his letters to Mum from Saugor on the verandah of his graceful, airy, detached bungalow, surrounded by a garden with flowers and trees. A watercolour of the bungalow and garden was painted for him by his friend, Major Hicks, at the end of September. It shows the shrubs and the elegant mohwa trees with their plum-coloured flowers.

The picture reveals another aspect of Dad's hopes. On the right is drawn the sturdy, wooden frame of a swing that he had put there in preparation for his first child's arrival.

And, a week after the watercolour was painted, I was born in circumstances far safer and more luxurious than anything ever enjoyed by any member of my parents' families in any generation. I was lucky to arrive in Whincroft nursing home, on the edge of Dartmoor.

The stress of separation from Dad for so long before she could go to join him in India and the burden of caring for her brothers and sister-in-law and of nursing Ted were taking their toll of Mum's health. The doctor attending her called her 'the excitable lady from Plympton'.

A month after my birth Mum received her first and only passport. It records her details:

        height – 5' 10";
        colour of eyes – brown;
        colour of hair – brown;
        special peculiarities, ——;
        British Subject by birth;
        wife of British Subject;
        one child;
        countries for which this passport is valid –
           British Empire.

The adventure in India was to be Mum's only travel abroad. She must have been nervous. An old friend, Vi Luxon, and with her a regular worshipper at the early 8am Holy Communion at St Mary's, gave Mum a beautifully illuminated card, kept for ever in the Family Bible:

> ... Renew our faith that we may feel Thee near
> Lest we forget Thee in our childish fear;
> Amid the turmoil let us know Thy Will
> And hear Thy tender whisper, Peace, be still.

At the beginning of January 1946 Dad was appointed M.B.E. (Military Division) in the New Year's honours list. Brigadier Cameron, his commanding officer, wrote to him that it was 'for a job well done'.

On the 10th of January 1946 Mum took a taxi from number 7 Stone Barton. She collected her sister Hilda at number 84, and then her brother Wally at his house on Plymouth Road. The two of them came with us on the train from North Road station in Plymouth to see us off at Liverpool docks.

On the twelfth, Mum embarked for India. She had to share a cabin with a mother and her twelve-year-old daughter, both of them selfish and unhelpful. Mum was afraid whenever she had to leave me on my own with them for a few minutes. They stole a brooch that Dad had given her. We disembarked at Bombay (now called Mumbai) on the 1st of February.

※

Fifty years later Mum wrote:

> I left Stone Barton for India ... the family coming to Liverpool on the train – first class. Leaving them to go on the ship – the Drottningholm, a Swedish vessel. A month's travelling – arriving at Bombay and meeting Jack, with John in the pram, and staying with friends of Jack's – then travelling to Saugor after riding around Bombay in a tonga.
>
> Train to Saugor – arriving at the bungalow and saying, 'Will I have to whitewash the ceiling?' (a joke!) – a huge room. Happy times at Saugor – lovely garden, birds and flowers. John growing all the time ... then leaving to come home when John was two.

Mother also wrote, on another occasion:

> I've just remembered our lovely bungalow in India. The garden was filled with flowerbeds and a great many tubs of roses, and a lovely birdbath in which parakeets of every colour bathed, and golden oriole and hoopoe. The mali [gardener] used to keep the flowers well watered. We had two bearers – Kalloo and Kundan – and a cook. A little boy used to pull the punkah [fan] to keep air flowing through.
>
> We went for walks early morning and late evening. The trees were lovely, covered in flowers. On one morning walk we saw a cobra, and Margo, our lovely white bull terrier, chased it. Dad threw a stone at it and it slid down a hole; apparently the insects irritated it and it came up to get cool and the eagles took

it ... We also had a beautiful white pony named Joey ...

Another night Dad went to kneel down beside our bed to say his prayers and he noticed a giant poisonous scorpion there, just in time. He took his shoe and managed to kill it.

Life was full of the kind of dangers unknown to a country girl from Devon. Mum found it difficult to adapt to an alien life. She could not change like a chameleon to match her circumstances. This immutability, in her case, was so bound up with her integrity and resolution that it saved us all in the long run; we would have sunk without it after Dad's ill health became critical, and then in the years after his death. But it must have made life difficult in smaller things, especially in India. Dad was more able than anyone to appreciate and enjoy Mum's ingenuous enthusiasm and eccentricity. His detached, wry good humour helped her not to take life too seriously, which was perhaps her way.

There were a good number of people whom Mum recalled with gratitude and affection. Colonel 'Tug'

Thornton, who used to soak up his gravy at dinner with a piece of bread; Joan Forteath, wife of another colonel, for whom she made Cornish pasties; Molly Stacey, wife of a major, who said to her, 'Go on, Grace, pick him up,' when I was crying in my cot. All of them helped her to cope. There was her delight in nature, her interest in the flowers, birds and animals, and, in fact, in all the different races and religions represented in the Army, like the bearded Sikhs and the tall, proud Pathans whom she caught sight of when she took me in the pram on the road around the practice ranges at the Small Arms School.

Then there was her music, the officers' ball, and the parties held at various bungalows. Mum was a gifted pianist and used to accompany others. Once, at a party, she suggested to the officer she was playing for that they perform the sentimental ballad 'Trees'. 'Spare me that, Mrs Symons, spare me that,' he replied, and his dry response raised Mum's spirits whenever she thought of it, even on her deathbed.

Many pieces of sheet music, stamped 'Rose and Company, Fort, Bombay (telegrams "Rosebud Bombay")', made their way to her in those days at Saugor: the *Destiny Waltz* by Sydney Baynes (2 rupees), *Bells Across the Meadow* by Albert Ketelbey (2 rupees, 8 annas), *Nights of Gladness* by Charles Ancliffe (2 rupees).

There was St Peter's church. Dad and Mum used to take it in turns to attend the Holy Communion service at eight o'clock on Sunday mornings, leaving the other to stay in the bungalow with me. By this time Tony Lawrance had returned to England from his seven-year chaplaincy at Saugor, to become the rector of Barmston on the Yorkshire coast, south of Scarborough and

Bridlington. Dad continued to tend his wife's grave at Saugor as long as he was in India.

Was Mum happy?

I think so. Although, in her words, she felt 'a fish out of water' at times, she suffered such feelings throughout her life. They were not any stronger while she was involved in the life of the Indian Army. Most important of all, she laid down many happy memories on which she would feed for the rest of her life.

Was Dad happy? I am sure he was. You can see it in his face in the photograph that shows him holding me in his arms outside his bungalow in February 1946, just after we had all arrived in Saugor from Bombay.

I am happy too, held firmly in his strong hands, peaceful and content in his embrace, as he looks towards Mum, taking the photograph, with a broad, untroubled smile and an unfurrowed brow.

But now there was a new source of great urgency, straight after the efforts of the War. Mr Attlee's government announced that India would be granted independence and later, reluctantly, that the subcontinent would be subjected to partition and that India and Pakistan would become two separate, independent states at the end of 1947. That date was later brought forward to the 15th of August of that year. The existing Indian officers were promoted and others commissioned, so that they would be ready for an orderly transfer of authority within the Army. Everything happened in a rush, and there was no time for Dad to take Mum to Pachmarhi, so she never saw his 'spiritual home in the hills'.

Because of Dad's modesty, Mum probably did not fully take in, at that time, what he had achieved and contributed to the Army at Saugor in those years. It was all much too strange for her. Later she understood better. Nonetheless she was wholly aware of his other qualities, and she too sensed later on that, after their return to England, he was not always appreciated for what he was and for what he had achieved. Many others experienced this on their return Home. Mum always specially liked those who valued Dad's modesty and humility, but who also saw beyond these qualities and appreciated him even more highly for himself and for his achievements.

This fear of Dad's not being valued, for all that he was and did, became an open wound for her later when he was in his fifties and sixties and Huntington's devastated him. Huntington's makes people want to hide themselves, or what has become of them, from others. It makes others want not to know you. See it, and you will understand.

As 1946 and 1947 passed, Dad filled his buff notebooks with preparations for the return to England and with information about the possibility of retirement from the Army.

At the end of 1946, in his last annual report on Dad, Colonel Gray wrote: 'A first class administrative officer. A most conscientious and reliable man in every way. One can thoroughly rely on any work he is given being done most thoroughly and efficiently. Has foresight, imagination and the power of getting good work out of his subordinates. Popular with all ranks, but a strict disciplinarian.'

Brigadier Cameron, commandant of the Infantry School at Saugor and well known among his contemporaries as a commander of the highest quality, who made great demands on his officers, added this final comment on the last day of December 1946: 'A first class administrative officer who has given unreservedly of his very best in his appointment as admin officer/Infantry Weapons Wing/Infantry school. I entirely agree with his CO's remarks.'

Both men graded Dad as 'above average' and recommended him for his next promotion. They offered him a regular commission in the British Army back at Home but he decided to take retirement, after twenty-eight years as a soldier. In his report in 1946, Colonel Gray records that, in their conversation about what he might do after retiring from the Army, Dad mentioned his interest in 'farming, gardening and social work'.

Dad began to make detailed lists of all that they had to send back to England. It amounted to enough to fill eight heavy teak boxes, each of them four feet by three feet by three feet in size, which he and Mum would pack, beginning in April 1947, for the journey Home. The luggage would carry the belongings that he had gathered over half a lifetime.

On the 9th of September, Dad entrusted Margo, our bull-terrier, to Kundan. For fifteen or more years he used to send money orders to Kundan and Kalloo when he wrote to them giving news of our life in England, and, with the help of letter-writers, they used to send him some news of the new India.

We made our way by railway to Bombay. The subcontinent was in turmoil.

On the eighteenth of the month, after spending twenty-five years and six months there – the vast bulk of his adult years and, at that time, well over half his life – Dad left India for ever, sailing with Mum and me from Bombay to England on the liner Strathnaver.

※

Like the Roman centurion who had served in the army so long in Britain that he could not bear the thought of leaving it and returning to Italy as the Roman Empire weakened and retrenched, Dad had loved India.

> Legate, I come to you in tears – My cohort ordered home!
> I've served in Britain forty years. What should I do in Rome?
> Here is my heart, my soul, my mind – the only life I know.
> I cannot leave it all behind. Command me not to go!

Now we were gone.

Dad's life could in any case never be the same again; but far worse than that loss, something happened to him on the voyage Home, something that would not be known to me for sixty years.

18
Making a Home

DAD OFTEN SPOKE TO ME of the horrors of Partition in India.

Some Indians who have exercised a heavy responsibility for their country's government and security over the years since then, have also told me, sixty years on, of those terrible days, which trouble their memories as much as they sully the reputation of Mr Attlee's government and that of Lord Mountbatten, the last Viceroy. One of the wisest and most experienced of those Indians told me privately that, had it been possible to grant India her independence a year or two later, much bloodshed would have been avoided.

Dad was not sure that, even in that way, it would have been possible to avoid tens of thousands of deaths. In any case, there was no choice. Great Britain had been bled white by her role in the War. The other Allied Powers, the Soviet Union and the United States, each had a strong interest in the dissolution of the Empire. They had little care for or understanding of the human consequences for the peoples of India and Pakistan. They wished to divide and share the spoils, Stalin cashing them in for ideology and power and Roosevelt and Truman for political theory and business profits.

For the many who, like Dad, loved the Indian people and their land and had served there for so long, it was a tragedy that the British left the country in such a way.

※

In her notes made fifty years after the events, Mum wrote:

> Arriving in Bombay after a trying journey from Saugor – I was five months pregnant – heat and journey were trying on a troop ship.
>
> Arriving in England – journey down to Plymouth and Plympton – meeting Jack's family and mine again. Eventually obtaining a cottage at Venton, near Sparkwell. Happy times with Jack and John in the cottage.
>
> Going a second time to the Horrabridge nursing home. Hilda looked after Jack and John ... Travelled home to Venton cottage and Jack and John.

They called it 'Saugor Cottage'. It was built deep into the left side of the lane which, with its tall Devonshire banks and hedges, runs down from the village of Sparkwell to the hamlet of Venton.

Venton means 'spring' or 'well' in Cornish. Wells and springs can be places of magic, good magic, and so it was there.

And it is here that I have my first memory, as clear as the water of the spring. It is of Dad, wearing a jersey and corduroy trousers, and the trilby hat that returned with us from India in one of the black teak boxes. Dad is carrying two heavy, galvanised buckets down the hill to draw our water from the pump, fed by the spring at the foot of the lane. It is December by now, and there

I am, rolling down the hill a few of the logs that Dad has stacked so carefully beside the cottage. Dad fills the buckets and then we walk up the hill together, with my hand held securely, gently in his. Dad puts the buckets down carefully at the gate, and we walk down the hill again. Together we collect the logs and restack them. We do this often together. I love Dad.

Of course there was no electricity, and Mum sometimes cooked with an oven made out of a large biscuit tin standing on two little brick walls, over an open wood fire.

We had an Elsan chemical toilet, the contents of which Dad used to bury each week.

Once a week he travelled into Plymouth to do some shopping. He used to buy fish from the fishermen at the market on the quayside at the Barbican. Perhaps this simple, regular life served to remind him of his boyhood in Newlyn.

Dad used to buy an occasional pint of beer, or a bottle of Forest brown ale, at the Treby Arms in Sparkwell. The pub, with its comforting yellow, nicotine-stained walls, and with the same publican, survived unspoiled and unchanged for forty years. Mr Nelder, with his black moustache, shining bald head and courteous, quiet manner, remembered Dad all those years later. 'He was a gentleman,' he told me.

In the cottage, oil lamps with dark green or pink shades lighted our two rooms, one up and one down. There was a Claygate brick fireplace downstairs. We had roaring log fires. Two Christmas trees, so tall that they bent over against the ceiling, were surrounded by toys. The postman, delivering parcels, commented to Mum that it looked like an enchanted land. It was.

The rent was only fifteen shillings (75p) a week, because the steep bank of earth supporting a hazel and hawthorn hedge at the back of the cottage were giving way, and it was Dad's responsibility to deal with that problem. He employed Mum's brother Jack, who earned his living as a jobbing gardener, to build a dry-stone wall there.

This was as much an act of generosity on Dad's part as a necessity. Congenial work was hard to find in Plympton. In the tiny notebooks in which Dad, in his beautiful, neat hand, kept his accounts in the 1940s and 1950s, there are entries indicating his occasional subsidies given to some member of Mum's family, even after it became necessary for him to manage his money very carefully. I am struck by the extent of his generosity to a few of her relatives, hidden away in these books.

By the middle of January 1948, when my brother was born, the primroses were already flowering in the Devonshire hedges. Mum wrote:

> Our walks, picking flowers and sticks together to light our lovely fire ... food rationed and therefore enjoyed more as a treat.

At the end of the month my brother was baptised at Sparkwell church, and in February we moved away.

Perhaps through some Army connection, Dad applied for and was appointed to the position of estate manager at Thoresby Hall in Nottinghamshire. It looked a good prospect. Farming and gardening, together with social work, were the occupations he had mentioned as interests for work after retiring from the Army at the time of his final report with Colonel Gray in Saugor. Mum's family on her mother's side had originated in that part of the English Midlands.

As we travelled north in the train, the primroses in the hedgerows gave way to the grime and soot of the industrial Midlands and the coalfields of Nottinghamshire. If Mum had had any romantic feeling about returning to her mother's roots, they soon disappeared. She hung out the washing in the dark mists of a hard winter and took in the clothes grimy with coal-dust.

The weather was especially harsh for Dad after so many years in the tropics, with no chance gradually to get used to the temperatures and the raw dampness in England.

We were living in a flat above the stables, and one day I nearly fell through the window. The pane of glass that I had knocked out of the frame hit a woman walking in the yard below. Only her thick hair protected her from a serious injury. Mum wrote:

> There were thirty-two stone steps up to our flat, which was like a hospital – long passages. It was a converted stables at Thoresby Hall ... We had to share the flat with a young lodger who was not a very likeable chap. When we opened the window, coal-dust from a nearby mine blew in. Memories of Nottingham not good, I'm afraid.

The single happy memory from that time was when Dad and Mum took us to Sherwood Forest and we stood inside Robin Hood's 'Major Oak'. There seems to have been no chance to find a better place to live, and it is not clear that Dad was enjoying the work.

So Dad and Mum decided to move to Cornwall. For a while, Dad's pension would be enough for us to live on. They thought that St Ives would be ideal for the four of us.

Dad travelled down to Penzance by train. He visited Newlyn and stayed with his family. He found a bungalow, then called 'Maginot', one and a half miles to the west of the centre of St Ives and eight miles to the east of Land's End.

On his return, he told Mum the news that there were few houses available at that time, and he showed her the careful drawings of the bungalow and its garden that he had made.

Mum was overjoyed about the house and the garden.

We moved to Cornwall in the middle of June and they renamed the bungalow 'Babworth', the name of a country house, not far from Thoresby Hall, where Mum's parents had once been in service. Mum wrote:

> The journey to St. Ives via Paddington – Uncle Jack Aldersey and Auntie Nellie's present of food for the journey to Cornwall. Travelling first class, under Jack's pension arrangements for one year.

On part of the journey from Paddington we shared a compartment with the Duke of Portland who was shrewd enough to praise 'the boys' to Mum. She always remembered his beautiful leather luggage, inscribed with K.G. after his name, in gold leaf.

For Dad, too, it was a happy return. He was devoted to his sisters, and all his life he felt a special responsibility for his youngest sister, Kathleen.

The mild climate in west Cornwall was perfect for Dad. Despite his time in India Dad did not feel the need to wear his blue tweed overcoat at all during our two years at St Ives.

He loved to work in the garden. He kept a few fowls for eggs. I played alongside him. Together we cleaned out the chicken house. I did my best to help him in the flower garden, pouring water over the granite birdbath and rocks that lined the flowerbeds and watching it mysteriously steam up on the sun-baked stones.

Behind the bungalow was a field where the local farmer grew swedes and cabbages. When Dad and I were there on our side of the hedge, working together in the chicken run, the farmer would pass by on his tractor, which had only recently replaced two heavy shire-horses. On his way home to his midday dinner, he would call out to us, 'See 's af'noon!'

My first memory of Mum is the image of her cooking pasties in the biscuit-tin oven over an open fire kindled between two rows of bricks in the back garden.

It was a happy time for her, too. She wrote:

> Bonfires in the garden at St. Ives;
> cooking in the garden;
> times on the beach, building sandcastles;
> visits from all the family, and walking over the cliffs and climbing down to the sea and being among the rocks;
> lovely picnics at a sort of tor quite near our bungalow.

Dad was planning our future. He knew the value of schools and learning. I feel it when I dip into the books that he gathered over the years in India, especially the set texts, anthologies and grammars that he used when, in the early 1930s, he studied for his Higher National Certificate.

The photograph that Florence Louisa gave him for his fourteenth birthday shows him and his fellow pupils, some sitting and some standing, in well-ordered rows in front of their classroom. The school looks neat and tidy, well run and careful of its pupils, but it was small and limited in what it could offer them.

Schools in west Cornwall had not changed much in forty or fifty years. Dad felt it would be best to move to Plympton, which had a good grammar school. Florrie's children had attended it; in fact, they had shown it to Dad when its new building was being constructed during his home leave in 1936. Then, there were other good schools in Plymouth, twenty-five minutes away by bus.

Dad also knew that he must get a job to provide us with an adequate income. This would be easier near Plymouth. The post-war inflation was already eating into his precious pension and savings.

Dad went to Plympton for a few days and lodged there with Hilda and Fred. With their help, Dad found a house. It was in a quiet road, lined with lime trees and lilac bushes. Behind it stretched a lush green field, safe and open for children to play.

The house, number 10 Moorland Road, was only fifty yards from the high street, called Ridgeway. It was ideally placed in the village, on the bus route to Plymouth, near the shops, the library, the primary school and the doctor's surgery.

Number 10 was part of a mid-Victorian terrace, built in 1867, with a secluded walled back garden. The front garden and the sitting-room faced west.

Before we moved in, Dad arranged for a Rayburn to be installed in the kitchen, for cooking and hot water, and for the bathroom to be fitted out afresh.

On a damp, drizzly, rather muggy day in August 1950, we left St Ives. We said a sad goodbye to Miss Date, the local shopkeeper, who gave us home-made pasties, wrapped in white napkins, to eat on the train. 'She is an honest, kind woman,' Bernard Leach, the potter, had told Dad when we had moved in. His studio was just down the road from 'Babworth'.

We stood on the platform of St Ives station with our luggage: each of us had a small suitcase. I wore a navy gabardine mackintosh and a cap. We passed through damp, misty countryside, eating Miss Date's pasties. Nearly three hours later we rolled across Brunel's bridge over the River Tamar and entered Devon. We skirted the dockyard at Devonport. There were glimpses of some of the ships of the Royal Navy, and then of the city of Plymouth, still in ruins from the blitz.

We caught a taxi to number 10 from North Road station in Plymouth, although at that date there was still a station in Plympton. Dad opened the green, wooden gate into the garden, protected from number 12 and the road by a privet hedge. There was no hedge between the small, adjoining lawns in front of number 10 and number 8.

With a Yale key, unchanged in all our years there, Dad unlocked the heavy green front door and led us into a lobby, the inner door of which was glazed with Victorian glass panes – blue, green, dark yellow and red – through which the setting sun would cast its peaceful light on us, like a spell, for fifty years. He opened the glass door, and we were in a long passage, rather shabbily decorated with fawn wallpaper, but graced by an elegant banister and staircase. On the right was a large sitting-room, with a bay window looking on to the front garden, and a dining-room with a tall window giving on to a slate path leading to the back garden. Both rooms had tall, marble fireplaces – white in the sitting-room, black in the dining-room.

We walked along the passage to the kitchen and scullery, beyond a small lobby with a door designed to allow the Victorian proprietors to enter the garden without passing through the kitchen and scullery, the domain of their servants. When the house was built, there would probably have been a cook and a housemaid working there, the sort of work done by Mum's mother in her first years in service.

Together we explored the rooms upstairs. There were three bedrooms, a dressing-room next to the front bedroom, and a bathroom. The bathroom and back bedroom, the kitchen and scullery below them, with a larder and coal cellar, formed a tenement jutting out into the back garden, which was bordered by a stone wall six feet high. A wooden door led into the back lane. The garden was dominated by a lilac bush, big enough for us to make a primitive tree house, and an enormous 'New Dawn' rose-bush.

In September Dad set about finding a job. At the same time, I started school in the infants' class, in the room in which Mum had herself begun to attend lessons a few weeks after the outbreak of the First World War.

We owned number 10 for fifty years.

These decisions and plans of Dad's turned out to be almost his last, great initiatives for us all. Everything depended on them, and they successfully set the pattern of our lives for so long.

Only now do I know how costly they must have been, how draining of his mental resources. For, hidden from him and us, within every cell of Dad's body, things were on the move.

19
'Huntington's explains it all'

IT BEGAN WITH Kathleen.

Before the War, Kathleen had lived with her sister Clara and brother-in-law Charlie. At the end of her war-work in the aircraft factory in Gloucestershire, she moved back to Newlyn. For some years she lodged with Nora and Reg and their six sons.

Kathleen began to work at a guesthouse in Penzance, and often brought home some of the unused food that was going to waste at the end of the day. Nora's sons remember the treats that Kathleen brought them, like trifles and fruit salad. In those days, in the late 1940s, food rationing was even more severe in Great Britain than it had been during the war. Despite that, we continued to send supplies to Germany where the population was on the verge of starvation.

It was in the late 1940s that Kathleen began to be affected by Huntington's.

'She got the shakes and jitters,' one of Nora's sons told me. 'We laughed at her.'

And across all the time that has passed since those

days, so many years, you can hear the shame and guilt and confusion and embarrassment in his voice.

'We didn't understand,' he told me. 'We were too young.'

And how could they possibly understand? How could they know?

For Kathleen was the first in her generation to be affected. All of Nora's six sons had been born long after her uncle Frank had died of Huntington's in 1921. Not one of them had seen it. How could they know or guess?

After Dad's death in 1972 I also began to be troubled about Auntie Kath. Had I been unkind to her? Had I made things worse for her? Had I made Dad unhappy by doing anything that upset her?

Huntington's is a disease of families, even happy ones, as well as of individuals.

A couple of years after Kathleen became ill, Clara's health began to go down hill as she slowly developed the first symptoms. Four of Clara's five children developed the disease and died of it. Barbara, who has been spared, recalls that, at around the age of ten, in 1952, she first became aware, and consciously took in, that something strange was happening to her mother. In order to make up for the loss of what her mother could give her, in attention and closeness, she somehow began to 'move over', as she puts it, to her father, so as to draw from him more of what all ten-year-olds need from their parents. Later she came to understand that, at that age, she had to protect herself by distancing herself from all that was happening to her mother.

There is something about the drop in energy and interest, the look of 'lostness' caused by Huntington's, that drives a child to do this, just to survive the pain caused by that feeling of loss. It happens; it is bound to happen. We were lucky to have two parents. Imagine what it would be like in a one-parent family. I dare not. God forbid.

And Dad was living there at St Ives with us, near Newlyn and Penzance, from 1948 to 1950, as this began to happen to Kathleen and Clara.

Dad had known his Uncle Frank. He must surely have learnt something of how his life had ended, although he was away from Newlyn during his last two years and, if you have not been involved in Huntington's, you will hardly believe how far we will go to hide the truth from ourselves and from those whom we love and want to protect. Florrie and Nora are likely to have known how Uncle Frank had died and probably they saw him in his last, most affected years. The other sisters were, perhaps, too young in 1921 to take it in, especially if Frank was being protected and kept out of view.

So when Dad saw what was happening to Kathleen and, a little later, to Clara, something would have stirred in his memory.

Once you have seen it, you never forget it.

What Dad made of it, who can tell? Certainly he could have had no idea of its real significance. Ninety-five per cent of the doctors in the country were ignorant of that in 1950. But I suspect that some ill-defined anxiety crept into his mind. If so, was it an ordinary anxiety Dad felt, or was there already something more at work?

A couple of months before we moved from St Ives to Plympton, Florrie's son Terry and his fiancée Maureen, both in their early twenties, stayed with us for a week's holiday. It was June 1950, Terry told me. What difficulty Dad and Mum had in handling their two young sons, they thought. Perhaps it was just the trials of middle-aged parents, now forty-eight and forty years old, dealing with the energy of a four-year-old and a two-year-old, but Terry and Maureen were puzzled. Whether or not because of this experience, they settled for one child. But when, not long afterwards, he next saw Dad in the very early 1950s, Terry recalls a hesitancy in him, a nervousness and lack of confidence. His behaviour and manner were strikingly different from what he remembered of Dad at the time of his Home leave in 1936 and 1944, and completely at odds with everything in the detailed reports on Dad's confident manner and efficient work, written just four years earlier in India.

There is another witness to what was happening. At the wedding reception held at number 7 Stone Barton after Dad and Mum were married in 1944, Terry had been joined by Hilda's son, John, to sing some songs. Mum accompanied them at the piano.

John was fifteen years old at the time of the wedding. He has a vivid recollection of Dad at that time: very smart, with an upright bearing, clearly a military man, who spoke briefly and to the point. His description matches Dad's reports.

John left the grammar school at seventeen, in 1946, and he worked for a few months as a cub reporter on the local newspaper, the *South Devon Times*. Sixty years later he still had his reporter's eye, an objectivity and cool detachment. He was away from Devon on National Service between mid-1947 and May 1949. For nearly six years John did not see Dad. He met him again in Plympton in the spring of 1950 when Dad went to stay with Hilda and Fred for a few days while he was searching for a house for us to live in after our move from St Ives.

Immediately, John noticed a difference. Dad's speech was a little vague; his bearing was less upright and less military; he seemed somehow to have less control of the movements of his limbs and had begun to stumble and to drop things. At first, during those months in 1950, John thought that the reason for this change was that Dad was finding it difficult to adapt to life in England after spending so long in the Army in India. After all, it was bound to be a difficult change. Of course, John had never met Kathleen or Clara, so he had no reason to suspect that there was 'something in the family'.

John recalls that he talked about Dad with his parents at the end of 1950, in the weeks before he moved to Southampton. 'We were aware of something, but we didn't mention it to anyone else. We noticed that he was rather clumsy around the house. We thought he was missing the ordered life of the Army after so long.'

But somehow, even at the time, it seemed to John to be more significant than that. Dad was not as incisive as he had been; he was in some way 'bewildered'. And, with hindsight, John can see that what he was witnessing was the beginning of the slow development of Huntington's disease.

'That explains it all,' John said. 'It was the missing piece of the jigsaw. It makes sense of everything else; of all the things that we could explain away on their own and put down to the effects of India or premature ageing because of the hot climate, or a lack of practical dexterity, or late fatherhood ...

'Huntington's explains it all.'

For a while, after John told me of his memories of 1950, it seemed that there was no one to tell me more of what happened in those years, no one who had been old enough at the time to see what was happening and was still alive with reliable memories.

Then, not long after the death of Auntie Edie's daughter, my cousin Mavis, I telephoned her brother Gerald, who had by then lived in Canada for over thirty years. Mum had told me that he was a most interesting and kind person, and that she always enjoyed seeing him and talking to him on his visits from Canada.

Gerald had served in the army in India at the end of the Second World War, from 1944 to 1947. He read widely and was well informed about many things. He was blessed with the powerful memory for places and people that seems to come down the line of the Aldersey family, through Mum's mother.

Gerald told me that he had vivid memories of his only meeting with Dad. He had visited us at Venton Cottage in his Morris Cowley motor car only a month or so after we arrived back from India. He had been demobilised in April 1947 and had used his 'demob' money to buy a car, first an Austin Seven and then the Morris. He was twenty-one years old.

It was the autumn, probably late October or early November. The evenings were drawing in. Gerald had taken his mother, Edie, out for a drive in the country that afternoon and Edie had pointed out to him the signpost to the hamlet of Venton. Gerald had suggested that they call in on us. Edie warned him, 'You may get a surprise when you see Uncle Jack.' Gerald did not understand what to make of this.

It was a lovely visit, Gerald told me. He parked in the

narrow lane outside the cottage. While Mum and Edie were talking together and I was playing on the carpet, he had an interesting talk with Dad about India, part of it in Urdu. Gerald had visited Peshawar, Razmak, Meerut, Rawal Pindi, Derha Dun, Poona and Bihar before being moved to Siam (Thailand). He and Edie stayed with us for a couple of hours.

Gerald's work took him away from home a good deal, and then he emigrated, so he never met Dad again.

Gerald recalls that perhaps as many as a dozen times during the visit, Dad was affected by 'spasms'. As he sat in a big armchair, one of his shoulders or the other would inexplicably jerk upwards; one of his feet would leap a little from the floor by about three or four inches. Two or three times his body leant or twitched forward and back.

The first symptom he noticed stuck clearly in Gerald's memory. Dad's right arm rose suddenly above his shoulder, 'in the way children raise their hands in class to ask for permission to go out of the room to the toilet'. When this happened, Gerald jerked back into his own chair in surprise and he was afraid that this reflex reaction might have offended Dad. He began to feel that Dad was aware of what was happening and felt that Gerald was 'staring at him'. Gerald was confused by what he saw and did not quite know how to behave. But Dad took a lot of interest in him and they had a good conversation.

Gerald told me that it was terrible to see someone so intelligent afflicted in this way, so soon after he had been fit and well at the wedding (according to Edie) less than three years earlier. He thought that it must be something like Parkinson's disease, and knew nothing of Huntington's.

On the way home in the car, Edie 'had a good cry'.

'Grace is such a lovely girl, and she has got a marvellous constitution and she is coping better than I expected,' said Edie. She dried her tears because she did not wish her husband Len to see that she had been crying.

Gerald had no idea who it was who had already seen Dad and had been able to warn Edie about the change in his health since the wedding. He remembers that he heard a little later, perhaps from Edie or Len, that 'something had happened' when we were at sea on the journey back from India in September 1947, and that Mum had had to call for medical help for Dad. Gerald wondered whether, suddenly and out of the blue, Dad had suffered his first 'spasm' during the sea voyage.

Who can tell, but it seems possible that it was on board ship, as he was returning to England to settle at Home after his twenty-five years' service in India, that Huntington's began to take its grip on Dad.

Whatever the truth of that, as Mum wrote to me:

There were so many happy times and memories at Venton and St Ives and number 10 Moorland Road.

20
Number 10

WE SETTLED INTO number 10.

On a Monday morning at the beginning of September 1950, Mum took me by the hand and, together, we walked down Station Hill for my first day's school. In the walls on both sides of the road grew pink valerian flowers and ferns, some light green, others like dark green lace.

The door opened on to the infants' class of Plympton County Primary School. The building was still rather battered from its service in the War as a government office, a little dark and forbidding with high ceilings and tall, narrow windows. Mrs Gardiner, the teacher, used to open them with an S-shaped brass hook fixed to the end of a long, wooden pole. She saw that I was subdued on my first morning at school, and she gave me a duster to clean and tidy a shelf. The atmosphere was peaceful, friendly and warm.

'He'll be all right,' Mrs Gardiner told Mum. Soon I was more than all right. I began to love school and learning, soaking up information and thoughts and impressions.

Mum began to work on making our new home. This is how she remembered it:

Taking the little boys to the babies' school at the bottom of Station Hill and Mrs Gardiner. Lovely times playing the games we bought for their birthdays; table tennis. Fireworks on Guy Fawkes' day – visits to Lee Moor to fire the big rockets.

Walks with the old push chair to Cadover Bridge. Trips in the train from Plympton station to Paignton zoo. Trips on the train to Princetown from Marsh Mills – picking whortleberries and mushrooms. One game – on the stairs playing buses, with Dad and me as passengers.

Lovely books Dad bought for them and reading stories. Parties in the dining room with lots of food on the big table. They had great times in the back garden, building a house in the corner and lighting a fire.

Our visits to Mrs Barnard's shop in Ridgeway to buy little toys and games.

Dad got a job. With the advice and encouragement of one of his friends from India, he was interviewed and selected to become a member of the War Office Constabulary, later known as the Ministry of Defence Police.

Dad was sworn in as a constable by Superintendent Hill during his training course at Didcot. He became PC 1484. While he was in training at Didcot Dad visited Uncle Jack and Auntie Nellie in London. He sent us cards and presents, bright red toy telephones.

After the month's training at Didcot, Dad came home and began to work at 'Coypool', a munitions factory and depot at Marsh Mills, about midway between Plympton and Plymouth.

His wages for the first week in January 1951 were £6 2s 6d, net of tax and other deductions. He worked a six-day week, with 24 days' leave (four weeks) a year. It was shift work, rotating week by week from early turn (6am to 2pm), to late turn (2pm to 10pm), and finally night duty (10pm to 6am). One week in three he had to catch up with his sleep during the day.

Quite often Dad had to work on Sundays. Occasionally he had a long weekend off duty, from 2pm on Friday to 10pm on Monday. But, as the notes that he made during the course at Didcot record, 'There is also a short weekend (from 6 o'clock on Sunday morning until 10 o'clock the same evening) which we shall not go too deeply into,' in Superintendent Hill's words.

The daily and weekly pattern of Dad's work established itself. It lasted twelve years.

※

Month by month in those years Dad kept an account of our income and expenditure. From his childhood he had learnt how to budget.

In his last years in India his fellow officers entrusted to him the handling of their mess-chits and bills. 'It was his integrity we trusted,' one of them told me.

Dad did the same for St Peter's church, Saugor, as church secretary and treasurer. Among the last cheques he signed in India was one for the church's quota assessment, to be paid to the Nagpur diocesan treasurer – 500 rupees, dated 3rd June 1947; and for 176 rupees he bought from the Saugor Mission one brown and two red rugs. The rugs remained in our dining room until we sold number 10, in November 2000.

Dad lived by his maxim, 'Take care of the pennies and the pounds will take care of themselves.' He was generous, but he knew, and taught me, that 'a fool and his money are soon parted'. 'Rupees – annas – paise,' he used to say to me, like a mantra. How urgent was his concern to provide for us.

Our budget was small. It was not helped by the state of the house, which the previous owner had allowed to run down. Number 10 often needed to be patched up.

From the neat columns of figures in Dad's small leather-bound account book, it is easy to see that he was carefully managing the budget to put aside money for our education later on. He and Mum succeeded in doing this by spending almost nothing on themselves.

In 1952 Dad's monthly income was about £30 from his Indian Army pension and a little less from his current work. He paid about £10 a month income tax and national insurance contributions, leaving a net income of about £600 a year. The records seem to suggest that Dad also paid a small amount of Indian income tax on his Army pension until the end of March 1955. His gifts of money, by postal order, to Kalloo and Kundan at Saugor, continued for long after that. Sitting in the armchair in the dining room, Dad used to read me their replies and tell me stories about their time with him and how they would be living now.

The net figure for his income may have risen to about £750 a year by 1963, when Dad retired. Of course, after his retirement it went down a lot. Mum said to me, 'We'll have to draw in our horns.'

In July that year, Mum's brother Wally nosily asked him, in my presence, about his income. We were just beginning the painful process of adjusting to living on Dad's Indian and War Office pensions. Wally asked Dad about his income before retirement, and Dad told him that it had never exceeded £1,000 a year. Wally seemed taken aback or perplexed by the answer, and that wordless response of his was a tribute to how Dad and Mum managed.

Dad's planning, and his and Mum's self-denial (like Dad's tanners from coal-heaving as a boy), saved us and, in truth, created much joy and happiness for the four of us.

※

Our daily happiness, at tea-time after school, was focused on 'Children's Hour' on the BBC Home Service.

> Between the dark and the daylight,
> When the night is beginning to lower,
> Comes a pause in the day's occupations,
> That is known as the Children's Hour.

As Mum recorded:

> Listening to Children's Hour, with David Davis and Violet Carson and Herbert Smith ... Wonderful serials and stories from our black Vidor radio set, by the Rayburn in the kitchen in winter and in summer out on the rickety table in the back garden at teatime.

Our annual happiness was centred on our caravan holiday. This became a tradition. It began in 1952 and lasted for fourteen summers.

Dad heard about Challaborough, a big sandy beach near Bigbury-on-Sea and Burgh Island in south Devon, from Mr Pascoe, a colleague at work. Mr Pascoe owned a caravan there and was willing to let it to us. In 1952 Dad paid him £5 for two weeks' rent of the caravan, and £3 to Mr Jeffrey, the owner of the local garage and taxi firm, to take us the thirty miles there and to bring us home in his black taxi, a comfortable pre-war Morris Ten. The car seats were upholstered in sagging dark blue leather and the car's huge chrome headlamps stood like pudding basins balanced on their sides on the front mud-guards.

In that first year there were only a dozen to twenty caravans at Challaborough, all parked to the west of the little stream that runs down the valley into the bay. This land belonged to the Crooks family, who had lived nearby for many years.

Mr Crooks also ran a small shop that sold bread and milk, newspapers and groceries, and a tiny café where Dad bought us wonderful milkshakes for 6d. We boys would take it in turns to go with Dad to the shop and café for this treat. For many years we could buy all our daily food with a ten-shilling note (50p).

Our caravan had plenty of ground to itself and a small garden, with a mountain ash tree. It was close to the stream that flowed quick and clear, bordered by sedge and reeds at its mouth. We lived there, the four of us, happily and peacefully for a fortnight.

We specially loved the weeks that we sometimes spent at the caravan at the end of August, stretching into the first few days of September, when the shadows lengthened after teatime and we swam late in the day. By 6 o'clock the tide had washed the sands clean and smooth and all was quiet; not that there was litter or many people holidaying there in the early days.

Sometimes we used to walk over the cliffs to Bigbury-on-Sea to the east, where Mum loved to play the penny-in-the-slot-machines, or to Ayrmer Cove, which we called the 'Magic Beach', to the west. But, apart from those outings, we felt no reason to leave the caravan site and the beach until Mr Jeffrey arrived to take us back to number 10, where we always remarked how long and green the front lawn had grown in our absence.

In August 1952 Dad made a note in his accounts that he spent £3 on 'Fred: taxi'. It was the start of another annual ritual.

Uncle Fred, with Auntie Hilda, would take us for a day's tour of beauty spots on Dartmoor. Mum packed our wicker hamper with Cornish pasties, and with apple pasties to be slit open and filled with clotted cream. We stopped, often at Dartmeet, for our midday picnic. Later, at teatime, Dad and Fred (whose love of dark brown tea was legendary) would cut out a sod of turf and make a bracken fire to boil the kettle and brew up.

The cars that Dad hired were magnificent Morrises or Austins from the 1930s; always they were black or dark blue. They held all six of us comfortably, with two of us sitting on the folding seats immediately behind the glass screen that separated the driver from the passengers. I sometimes took a turn to sit in front, next to Uncle Fred and felt very grown up doing this.

Mum wrote:

> One day Andrew White [an only child, whose family lived at number 6, two doors away from us in the terrace] was here, and as we loaded into the car and were squashed together with baskets of picnic food, he said 'Lucky pigs!' We could not squeeze anyone else into the car. It was strange, as when Andrew went in their car, a Morris Minor traveller, there was plenty of room; he seemed to want very badly to be jammed in with us.

Together with his parents and his grandmother Andrew and other children used to join us every Guy

Fawkes Night for our bonfire party in the back garden. Dad was in charge of the fire, and Mum would cook sausages and bake potatoes in the oven of the Rayburn. In the golden red light of the fire Dad would fork up pieces of flaming wood that fell out onto the path, and the adults used to sit on a bench by our coal cellar. When I met her, long after Dad's death, 'Nobby' Clark's daughter, Georgina, told me that Dad and Mum gave popular parties at their bungalow in Saugor. Each year, on 5th November, I saw a trace of that, the most sociable and exciting evening of the year.

※

In the early-1950s the Irish Republican Army waged a short and unsuccessful war of violence and terror in Great Britain. Coypool was an obvious target, and all the police officers were authorised to carry firearms. Dad was then still well enough to do so. He had been a brilliant shot in India, and only took to wearing reading glasses later in the 1950s. For some time he was able to cycle to work, but in 1953 he gave his bicycle to Uncle Charlie. From then he caught the number 21 bus to Coypool. Come rain or snow, he made that journey at all hours of day and night, until 1963.

Often I have wondered how Dad accepted the reduction in his level of responsibility. In India he had been accountable to the Brigadier for running the administration of the infantry weapons school. He had flourished. How did he now manage to find the grace to work under men who were often less educated and cultivated than himself? In fact, he enjoyed the company of his colleagues, all kindly men, many of them of his own age.

He found a wry amusement in observing them, as well as enjoying good companionship there. I now understand that this regular work gave Dad a strong framework for life at the time when his confidence and intellectual powers were under attack and gradually, very slowly at first, he was losing the steadiness and coordination of his limbs. One sergeant was a bully, but Dad coped with him, and that man was posted away.

It was Mum who, almost not knowing what she was implying, occasionally seemed to hint that this was all a sacrifice that Dad was willing to make for the three of us. From Dad there was no word of it.

21
At Risk

IN THE SUMMER OF 1953 Mum became ill. It seemed impossible. Mum wrote:

> We had not been living long at number 10. I was working quite hard with two small boys and the house to look after. I had 'housewife's tiredness' and my legs were very swollen. The doctors felt them and said that I must have three or four days in bed. It was summer time and the children were playing outside the house, in the garden. I was lying in bed with the windows wide open. Jack had time off to look after me. He used to bring me plates of meat and salad. The lady doctor said, 'Surely you are not going to eat all that?' Jack was so kind, and took great care of the boys. They were good, and I had a good time reading *Pride and Prejudice*.

Only a little earlier, at the time of the Queen's Coronation on 2nd June, Mum had still been in good health. There is a photograph, snapped on that day by one of Mum's friends, which she always kept in her handbag. It shows her looking bright and cheerful, and catches her face animated, with eyebrows raised and mouth half open in conversation. She found this silly look very amusing and always spoke of that day with great happiness.

After early-morning rain the sun broke through brilliantly in time for the tea and cakes, which Mum had helped to bake, and for the races, games and maypole. Dad was there. I remember how proud he and Mum were of our part in the games and the maypole dance, in which all the local children were involved and for which the boys wore white shirts and blue or red sashes, and the girls white dresses, specially bought or made for that day. There was cheerful, stirring music from a band conducted by Mr Howe, the director of the pit orchestra of the Palace Theatre, Plymouth. His daughter Sheila was in my class at school. It was a great celebration.

It gave me a curious stab of joy on 21st April 2006 to set a small Union Jack in the front window of our house to mark the Queen's eightieth birthday. All the memories and feelings of Coronation Day flooded back to me.

I pondered the words attributed to her mother when the Queen, then only ten years old, discovered how much her life would be changed by her father's accession to the throne as King George the Sixth: 'We must make the best of it.'

It is good advice, as wise for the one who will inherit the Crown as for those at risk from Huntington's. At a difficult time, Mum said to me 'Let's pretend that we are enjoying it, and that will help us do so.' Perhaps it comes to the same thing.

What was this 'housewife's tiredness' that overtook Mum so soon after Coronation Day?

A few years after her death, Dr Price, Mum's GP at the end of her life, showed me her medical records. He settled me in a little office in the corner of the surgery, and I made my way through the packet of folded papers. Dad's notes had been destroyed by then, so I never saw them.

The notes showed that Mum suffered from catarrh in mid-June and was prescribed codeine linctus. She must have felt seriously ill, because she always did everything she could to avoid visiting the doctor and she was suspicious of all 'tablets'. A month later she was diagnosed as suffering from oedema (dropsy) of the ankles. Her blood pressure was high and there was concern for her kidneys. By the end of the month the oedema was slight and it had disappeared by 6th August when we were able to go to the caravan for our holiday. While on holiday Mum developed curious sores on the palms of her hands, and it was only at the beginning of November that her hands were said in the notes to be 'almost cured'.

Mum had not seen a doctor between her second confinement, in January 1948, and mid-1953. She then consulted no doctor between 1953 and 1962, when for two months she had trouble with her varicose veins. So rarely did she visit the surgery that the doctors used to tease her about it.

I feel sure that Mum became ill in 1953, and was so run down during the second half of the year, partly because it was in these months that she understood more fully the seriousness of what was happening to Dad. She went through some sort of internal crisis.

In those days Kathleen was living in lodgings in the neighbouring village of Plympton St Maurice, about a mile from us at number 10. Plympton St Maurice and Plympton St Mary are linked by an ancient footpath, known as the 'Pathfields', shaded by an avenue of tall lime trees planted in 1897 to commemorate Queen Victoria's Diamond Jubilee. Every Sunday afternoon, Auntie Kath used to walk over to us, through the Pathfields, for tea. She used to take a weekly bath in our comfortable bathroom, supplied with limitless hot water by the Rayburn.

To my shame, I began to find her visits awkward as time passed. Now I understand how that happened. Gradually, Kathleen's unpredictable, irrational, choreic movements were becoming pronounced. The movements disturbed me, although I was not consciously aware of what it was that was troubling me. But for Mum, it was worse. She must have sensed, to some degree, that Dad was already on the same journey as Kathleen, not many years behind her, and that there could be no turning back.

How long was it before Dad realised that something horrifying was happening to him?

With all my heart, I hope that somehow Dad and Mum were protected from this knowledge, that it was years before they came to see the truth, but I cannot believe that it was so. Over the next two or three years they surely realised the true situation.

The mind takes extreme steps to conceal from us what it wishes to ignore, but eventually it surrenders to the truth. That is my experience, but not only mine. Dad was intelligent, observant and sensitive to other people and to atmosphere. He had been only five years old when his grandfather died; and he had been twenty, and away serving in the Army in Ireland, when his Uncle Frank reached the end of his life. The mind could easily push those events aside when Dad had so much to do that occupied and exhausted him, simply in order to earn his living, to survive and to help ensure that his frail mother and his sisters survived.

But now Kathleen and Clara were slowly changing. And above all, I fear, there was the look on the faces of the rest of the family and friends, however much they tried to control their reactions when they were with him. Their expressions, as time passed, must have confirmed to Dad the meaning of the loss of energy, the ebbing of interest, the 'bewilderment' from which he was beginning to suffer.

And what did he read in Mum's face? What did they say to each other?

In Mum's heart, surely, there came to be a fear, a dread, a growing conviction that she was losing Dad, inch by inch, day by day, and she could have had no idea of how or when it would end. My cousin Barbara tells me that she grieved almost more for the loss suffered by her father, Charlie, than for the terrible affliction of Huntington's that her mother, Clara, endured.

Then, for Dad and Mum, there was the horror of what all this might mean for their children. That was with them every moment of the day, and sometimes, I expect, in their dreams.

I feel sure that it was at that time, in mid-1953, that Mum began to see the similarity between Kathleen's advancing affliction and Dad's state, although it was then much less pronounced. If you are a member of an affected family and live every hour with a person suffering from Huntington's disease, those movements are unmistakable and terrifying. When, years later, out of the blue, you catch a glimpse of a sufferer out of the corner of your eye on a bus or a train, it is enough to tell you what is happening and you feel your blood run cold. What you feel for the affected person and anyone travelling with them – respect, pity, admiration for their coming out into the world – cannot be described.

Mum's physical constitution was robust. Even at the age of eighty-three she was described by a vascular surgeon as 'remarkably sprightly' as well as 'a delightful elderly lady, and happy in herself'. Dr Price, at the same time, referred to Mum's 'remarkable independence of spirit'. That is why I suspect that it was more than a physical cause that made Mum ill in 1953, when she was only forty-three years old.

What her two young nephews Gerald and John had successively seen, at its very beginning in November 1947 and then in early 1950, Mum now fully interpreted for the first time for what it was. She could no longer pretend it was not happening or was not significant. The horror of what she saw and sensed would be the outcome for Dad, and what she feared for their sons, worked its way through her system. The shock made her vulnerable to sickness and led to the oedema, high blood pressure and her hand infection.

Somehow Mum came to terms with what was happening. She regained her health by the end of the year.

※

Of course, I knew nothing of this threat. Mum and Dad took great care of us boys.

We still enjoyed life, the four of us as a family, in those years. It is good to remember some of the events of those days, and to handle again some of the presents that we received, even to look at theatre programmes from our outings together. Their value is so great because of what came later.

Dad took us to *Oklahoma!* and to *Rosemarie* at the Palace Theatre. We were all thrilled by the colour films of the conquest of Mt. Everest and of the Coronation, which we saw at the Royal cinema soon after those great events. We listened to *South Pacific* together on the radio one Saturday evening. We went on outings to Cadover Bridge and Princetown and Paignton Zoo. We attended the annual pantomime at the Palace Theatre.

In October 1953, Dad bought me a canary, 'Chippy', as my birthday present (15 shillings), and a light blue cage (£1 14s 6d). On his way back from work Dad would pick one or two pieces of groundsel for Chippy, bringing it home in the small brown case in which he carried his yellow and green sandwich tin, the book that he was reading at the time, and his torch. Then, when he ate an apple, Dad used to cut a slice and wedge it between the thin wire 'bars' of the cage, together with a piece of cuttlefish. I can see Dad doing it now, as gently as he could, with the occasional jerky, sudden movements of the arms that he was already developing. Mum told me that Dad used to hold Chippy carefully in his left hand and clip his nails with nail scissors. When Dad became really ill, at the end of our second canary's life, the little bird's nails grew long. Dad's hands were no longer steady enough to do that job.

In December that year Dad bought us each a 'crown' (a five-shilling piece) struck by the Royal Mint to commemorate the Coronation. We awaited the arrival of this present with great excitement.

As Spring arrived in February 1954, Dad bought a Conference pear tree, which bore beautiful and lavish fruit until Mum's death forty-four years later, when it too died. The tree cost 17s 11d, and it came from Chalice's nursery in Plympton, where Mum's brother Arthur had worked when he and his wife Edna were setting up their floristry business in the 1930s.

In March, Dad bought me a black Parker fountain pen, like his own, in preparation for my transfer to a new school in September. It saw me through Oxford and Cambridge.

After our holiday at the caravan in August, Dad's old friend Tony Lawrance, the padre in Saugor, visited us. With his second wife, Myrtle, he brought us a puppy, our first family dog. 'Patch' was a mongrel, half English bull-terrier, from the litter that the Lawrances had bred at Walkington, the village between Beverley and Hull in Yorkshire to which Tony had moved as Rector, after his years at Barmston.

In the same month Dad and Mum took me to Dingle's department store in Plymouth. They spent £33 (a fortune for them) to fit me out with what I needed for my first term at the preparatory school for Plymouth College.

For an eight-year-old, there was something exciting and curiously grown up about the smell of the uniforms in the schools department – sturdy wooden cabinets, displaying all the little blazers and short trousers, the rugby kit and gaberdine raincoats. In quiet groups, parents were gathered with their children, preparing for the autumn term and its games of rugby on the lush, green playing fields, marked out with sharp chalk lines.

In those weeks, Dad paid Mr Foale £30 to redecorate the hall, landing and staircase, which transformed the house for us. Unusually, that month's expenditure exceeded income by £30, and it did the same in September by £14. From time to time Dad was still lending or giving money to members of Mum's family (£1 in December, for example, to Hilda and Fred).

Soon after I started to attend the prep school in September, Dad had a short posting to Bridgwater. It may have been devoted to further weapons training, needed to secure Coypool during the IRA's campaign of terrorism.

During his time at Bridgwater Dad went up to London to visit Mum's Uncle Jack and Aunt Alice. Nellie had died and Jack had remarried. Like Uncle Jack, and Aunt Nellie before her, Alice took to Dad. The three of them attended the theatre in the West End, and Dad brought back some piano music for Mum, including *Getting to Know You*, from *The King and I*. Mum often played and sang this song.

This was Dad's last independent travel away from home. It was at home that he found his confidence with Mum and, I hope, with us boys. Later, in his early weeks at Moorhaven Hospital, he sometimes said, 'Take me back to number 10, Moorland Road, please.'

At Christmas, Dad and Mum gave me my first bicycle (£15 5s 6d, £15.27), green with three gears. My brother inherited my blue tricycle.

It had been an expensive year, but Dad knew what he was doing. In January 1955 he received a back-dated pay rise. As Mum often told me later, Dad came in one morning from night duty and, sitting on the edge of their bed, opened the fat pay packet, with £39 back-pay. Evidently I fully shared their pleasure at this: Dad let me write, quite neatly, 'Ha Ha! Ha Ha!' in his account book alongside that entry.

We all celebrated by attending *Cinderella* just after Christmas ('good,' Dad let me write in his notebook). The next day was my brother's birthday, for which he received a clockwork train set (£1 15s 0d). Hilda and Fred received another loan or gift of £1.

※

As the years had slipped by, Kathleen visited us less often on Sunday afternoons and then her visits stopped completely. Perhaps Dad and Mum had noticed that Kathleen's chorea was somehow unsettling me.

Instead of staying in for Kathleen, we started to go to Hilda's for Sunday afternoon tea. Dad did not often come on those visits to Hilda. I now realise that he used to stay at home so that Kathleen could call on him at number 10 to take her bath and spend some time with him there. Sometimes he visited her at her lodgings.

Kathleen became so unwell that she had to be admitted as a patient at Moorhaven Hospital for the rest of her life. Mum felt guilty about this. She so much wished to help her, but there was nothing she could do. Kathleen's condition, and its still faint and hazy reflection in Dad, must have been difficult to bear.

Dad was devoted to Kathleen. He often visited her at the hospital on his day off. What he saw happening to her must, in itself, have affected him deeply. There were also the fears for Mum and his sons, as well as for his own health.

In 1962 Dad arranged for a simple, beautiful grave for Kathleen, made of red granite. The inscription on the headstone in St Mary's churchyard reads: 'In God's keeping.'

She was forty-nine years old.

※

Quite soon after the New Year in 1955, when we went to *Cinderella*, I seem to have begun to sense more strongly – I was now well into in my tenth year – what was happening to Dad. Mrs Gardiner, at the infants' school, had told Mum that I absorbed things like blotting-paper. It was at the same age that my cousin Barbara took in what was going on in the case of her mother Clara.

At the end of the winter, in March 1955, we boys caught mumps. My brother quickly recovered, but I developed unexplained 'complications'. As a result, I missed the whole of my first summer term at the preparatory school and then stayed down to repeat that year. The medical notes report that I was anxious because I had heard Dr Owen say that, if Dad caught mumps, 'It could be serious for him at his age.' My anxiety must have been severe, for Dr Owen prescribed phenol-barbitone, and a consultant pediatrician visited number 10 to examine me. The consultation cost four guineas.

During those four months at home, often in bed, I studied Dad's two Hindustani text books and became quite fluent, writing in the cursive Urdu script that Dad used. I kept a diary in the script. It is a sign of my closeness at that time to Dad and his interests. He kindled my love of languages. It was surely my growing sense of the changes taking place in him that caused this jolt in my health.

Somehow the penny had dropped. Dad was changing,

becoming less himself, less capable, less than the full person whom, as a tiny boy, I had known and still now loved so much; becoming more like poor Auntie Kath.

So I suffered a crisis, and, as Barbara explained, I began gradually to withdraw from him, just to protect myself from the unexplained, frightening changes.

My withdrawal must have been at least as painful for Dad at the time as it remains for me as I recall it now. 'How much he loved you boys!' Mum used to say to me.

It is a pain that will not go away. It has also been a means of staying close to him over the years.

In writing this book about him and his family, I have grown so close to him that it is as if I now know him as he was when he flourished.

22
The Two of Them, Together

DAD SAVED THE SITUATION when I was ill for so many weeks in the spring and summer of 1955.

He rented the caravan at Challaborough for an extra fortnight in June. There was hardly anyone else there, so early in the season. We had the beach to ourselves. The weather was wonderful.

On our Vidor radio, we listened to exciting commentaries on the tennis championships at Wimbledon. We were cheering on Jaroslav Drobny who had won the men's singles championship the previous year when he was already well over thirty years old, but in 1955 he lost in the first round. It was not his success in 1954 but his mysterious name and nationality (a Yugoslav, exiled to Egypt), and his age, that put us on his side. We played our version of tennis, as well as cricket, on the grass beside the caravan, and enjoyed the sea air and swimming.

Dad's plan worked. The time at the caravan in June, and the usual two weeks in August, revived us all. I recovered my health.

※

In December Dad bought an Ekco television set with a seventeen-inch screen.

From time to time, in the 1950s, I gained an inkling of how his commission in the Army had changed Dad's life. In those days BBC television used, each autumn, to show the Prime Minister's speech at the annual banquet of the incoming Lord Mayor of London. One evening Dad and I were in the sitting-room, by the coal fire, watching the grand scene in Guildhall, with all the guests in evening dress, at long tables elegantly laid with silver and glass. Dad was sitting with his legs crossed on the carpet, as he often did when we were on our own at home in the family, a throw-back, I liked to think, to life in the jungle. 'Soup – fish – joint – pudding – savoury,' Dad said, and repeated it for me, with a smile, recalling the monthly formal dinners that he enjoyed in the officers' mess for those few years. And he explained to me about savouries, such as 'devils-on-horseback', of which I had never heard.

It is a lovely evening, a time for just the two of us; Mum is helping my brother to get ready for bed. Just the two of us on our own, Dad and me, just how I like it. But as I sit there on the sofa and Dad is squatting on the hearthrug, I must be taking in the way in which he is changing; taking it in without allowing myself to acknowledge it.

Gradually the changes in Dad seep into my mind, so surreptitiously that I am not conscious of noticing them or identifying them for what they are. I just experience the external effects of what is happening deep within every cell of Dad's body. I slowly begin to take it for granted that Dad's movements are not exactly like those of everyone else, except for Auntie Kathleen's. A few years earlier I had seen the same thing in her when she used to visit us every Sunday afternoon.

So Dad squats on his haunches, and every so often, unexpectedly, he shrugs his shoulders or brings his knees together; he opens his eyes rather wider than usual and then relaxes them; his fingers twitch a little or come to rest at slightly unusual angles; his head occasionally lolls back a little before correcting itself. But all this is so slight, so sneaky that I do not realise what is happening.

Yet, unconsciously, I am taking it all in. And it is happening, and the disease is changing Dad's consciousness, his state of mind. He and I are already slipping apart, he and the rest of the world – not that I care about the rest of the world, – it's us, the four of us, whom I want to scream and weep and rage about: it's we three who love him, whom he loves (of course, in my head I know that all the others matter so much, too). So he and I are slipping apart, and in this life there can be no retrieval, no going back. And this unexplained slipping apart will lead to terrible mistakes on my part and unbearable sadness that can never end – not in this life, it can't.

So all this is happening, unknown to me, as Dad and I sit watching the Prime Minister, Mr Macmillan, speak in Guildhall, lamenting with his charming, lugubrious, effortless irony, which gives such comfort, that his job does not give him time to watch *The Lone Ranger* on Saturday afternoons. Whatever else we face, at least Dad and I, and Mum and my brother, can do that together sometimes.

※

At school I began to forge ahead. But my growing devotion to study was to become my way of distancing myself from what was happening to Dad, an escape from the inexplicable pain surrounding us all, more sharply year by year. I protected myself by closing my eyes, shutting my ears. The gradual loss of the one who had given so much joy steadily constricted me and contracted my life, as if it were throttling me. I could not breathe normally.

Our strong family life, the pattern that Dad and Mum had built, saved us because soon after this Dad's strength began to ebb more noticeably. The pattern was set – a good pattern, a steady, well-balanced pattern for our life together, but Dad's energy and initiative waned, slowly, so slowly.

You can see it in his handwriting in the last in the series of his little account books, begun in May 1952. By 1955 and 1956 his hand has become less tidy and graceful, contrasting distressingly with the neat, small script of earlier days and previous notebooks.

And then there is an undated entry, probably coming from some time between late 1954 and early 1956. It reads '£60-13s-2d Dr. Blu'. It was apparently replaced by an even larger sum, £98 14s 0d.

'Dr. Blu' seems to be an abbreviation. It seems almost certain that, in one way or another, there was a series of consultations with an extremely expensive specialist doctor. It is possible that Dad consulted him, clearly more than once, in Harley Street when he visited London and stayed with Uncle Jack and Aunt Alice in October 1954, during his training course at Bridgwater.

Dad also wrote in a small address book, in capital letters, the word FENTAZINE, a drug used at that time to diminish the delusions and other psychotic symptoms of Huntington's patients. Perhaps this refers to medication prescribed for Auntie Kath, and perhaps she and Auntie Clara went with Dad, or separately, to consult Dr. Blu. That might explain the size of the fees, and Dad would probably have paid their travelling expenses.

Whatever the details of these consultations, the certainty is that Dad's condition was now worsening. It is likely that he felt the need for the best information and advice from an expert, and there were few experts in Huntington's in those days. Perhaps he and Mum had been able to hope against hope until then for some sort of release from what was happening, but at some time between late 1954 and early 1956 that hope died.

By now, more members of Mum's family were noticing what was happening to Dad's health.

Mum's brother Wally noticed a pale reflection in Dad of Kathleen's much more advanced symptoms. Since we had moved to Plympton in 1950, we had seen quite a lot of his family. Wally's son Richard remembers that when he was seventeen years old, his father had told him that he thought that Dad was developing the same illness as Kathleen. He can date this accurately to a little before or a little after July 1955, when he left school. At around the same time, Richard was also told by his father, or Richard overheard him say, that Dad had 'gone to west Cornwall' to consult the doctors and medical records about Kathleen and Clara's deteriorating condition. Richard himself has no clear recollection of a time when Dad was really fit and well.

Others saw what was happening, especially the shopkeepers in Ridgeway in Plympton. It was a quiet high street in those days, as well as being the main road between Plymouth and Exeter. Plympton was still a village of about six thousand souls, and most people did almost all their shopping in Ridgeway. The shopkeepers were 'fixtures', staying for many years; they were our friends.

Mrs Pearce, the owner of the hardware shop, and Mum were good friends. In the mid-1950s she noticed that Dad was getting ill. 'He was always so nice to talk to – a gentleman. It was very sad to see him going like that, very sad. I first noticed it when I was speaking to him. He began to shake a bit. It began to affect his speaking; it made his voice falter. It was dreadful that he was ill for so long – dreadful.'

Susan Pearce, her eldest daughter and one year younger than me, also noticed it in the mid-1950s. She cannot remember a time when Dad was really well. Especially, she recalls Dad's uneven, unsteady walk, and that Mum 'was always there for him, holding his arm, steadying him if he lost his balance'.

That is how I remember it. They faced it, the two of them, together.

Mr Kelly at the grocery shop saw it too. In the early 1950s he was a commercial traveller for a wholesale grocer and he used to visit several shops in Ridgeway. At some time in those years, he noticed Dad's strange walk. 'You couldn't help noticing it,' he told me, almost as if, out of his affection for Dad, he wished that it had been possible not to see what was happening, and to see only the true heart of Dad. Mr Kelly had noticed his unsteady movements well before 1958, the year when he began to work full-time at Mr Rhodes' shop. He later bought the shop, and he and his wife ran it until 1980.

Mum and Dad did much of their shopping there, and the four of them became good friends.

Mr Kelly told me: 'You could tell that he was intelligent. But now he was limited in what he could do. It was as if he couldn't manage any longer to use all his intelligence. His speech was a bit slurred and his vocabulary was a little limited, but he had all his faculties. We used to talk about everyday things.

'He kept his mind focused on what he was doing at the moment. He used to have a list from Mrs Symons of what he had to buy. His walk was uneven, with some long strides, then short ones, as if he were avoiding the cracks in the pavement, and then he would sometimes hesitate before walking on. He was always on the move and sometimes staggered. We knew, of course, that he hardly drank anything, but his gait made him look drunk. It was his walk that I noticed first.

'He was a gentleman, such a nice person, and it was such a sad ending after his career. He was kindness itself, and people respected him. It was very sad – they were both such nice people.'

Mr Kelly added: 'It was as if he was sorry to be inflicting the condition he was in on the people he met. Your Mum was a gem for him. She helped him keep occupied. They were a devoted couple.

'Your Dad took to Mrs Kelly and me and we used to talk. We were good friends. He had a lot of knowledge and he was interesting to talk to. Then he would lapse into silence and go on his way.'

Mr Kelly remembered, too, how sympathetic our neighbours at number 8 (Walter and Nancy Pearse) were about Dad's affliction when they visited him to do their shopping. The Pearses once told me that they felt that, because of what happened to Dad, they had never known him.

'I remember your mother', another neighbour from those years said to me, but her tone of voice changed immediately when I asked about Dad. 'It was nearly fifty years ago,' Mrs Gray said. How could I blame her? She, too, averted her eyes from what was happening. Yet, for many years Dad gave regularly to the British and Foreign Bible Society, for which Mrs Gray's husband, a clergyman, worked in Plympton, from 1953 to 1956.

Mary Davis, another neighbour, took in more of what was happening. Mary lived around the corner from us, in one of the comfortable, detached houses built in the 1950s, whose red brick Mum admired so much. Mary became one of Mum's dearest friends in later years.

She told me: 'Unfortunately, I never really came across your father. I don't recall ever talking to him. Your mother and I would talk at your front garden gate, and I got the impression that he was sitting in the kitchen. When Andrew [Mary's son] went through the house to play with you in the back garden, he told me that he saw your father sitting there – he was "tall and quiet and nice", Andy told me.

'I never really saw him or had the chance to have a talk with him. At first I just assumed that he was very quiet and retiring, but as time passed I felt that it must be something to do with his health. I just felt that something strange was happening.'

This invisibility to others, this non-existence that overtakes those with Huntington's, adds another sort of sadness to those who love its victims.

So, through the 1950s, this perception that something terrible was happening to Dad spread from the family to friends and acquaintances.

I lived too close to it all to take it in. I explained everything away in order to make the strangeness of it all bearable, to keep my balance.

I was lucky to have those years of not knowing.

I had no idea of what was happening, and I am glad.

23
Interlude

THIS IS MY PARENTS' STORY, the story of two lives and one marriage, but the constant presence of this dread, this sense of being at risk from something you cannot understand or change, is so difficult to understand that I will try to explain it from my own experience.

One Sunday afternoon in September 2002, I was driving on the A361 road between Devizes and its junction with the A4, near Avebury and Silbury Hill. It was a beautiful autumn day, with the golden sun lying quite low over the fields that stretch northeast to the Marlborough downs.

Something was familiar, but not immediately obvious. After a while, I realised what it was. I thought: 'This is the road on which I used to travel on my way back to Oxford at the end of each vacation between 1966 and 1968.' I used to pull the Morris Minor into a lay-by where the road ran past the edge of a copse of alder trees beside a little lake, and there my brother and I would eat the Cornish pasties that Mum had cooked for us for the journey. Not many cars would pass us while we ate. The road was quiet in those days.

And for the next few minutes, as I remembered all this, so many years later, in a deep silence, I experienced again what it used to be, to live without the risk of Huntington's.

The stillness and the empty road and the steady motion of the car and the recollection of that lay-by with its alder trees and the view across the open country to the Downs, which I had not seen for nearly thirty-four years, cast a spell on me. I was free.

The spell held me and comforted me as long as I was on that road. It was broken as soon as I turned onto the A4, on which I have driven once or twice since I learnt from the doctor that I was at risk on the twenty-sixth day of February 1969.

This is the only time in the years since those days that this sensation of freedom, of all the generosity of life and its possibilities has flooded into my consciousness.

And so I learnt afresh from those few minutes the pattern of what Dad and Mum went through.

For so long they knew that something terrible was afoot. And the knowledge that it was happening could never wholly leave them, yet they did everything for us. That is the measure of their courage and faithfulness.

They bore the knowledge and dread on our behalf as long as they could. They did us a great good. Together they enabled my brother and me to live so long knowing nothing of that risk.

Love is the meaning of it all.

24
No Way Out

DAD WAS NOW in the second half of his fifties, and some sort of crisis was smouldering, for him and for all four of us. He was gradually slipping into the background. I shut my eyes and directed my mind elsewhere.

Only once more was there a big event – important for me, that is – which Dad decisively affected. In the summer term of 1959, he visited 'HD' (Hugh Dent), my form master at the College, and discussed with him whether I should begin to study German or ancient Greek when I moved up to the third form in September.

By now it must have been a great test for Dad to do this for me. There was always something painful and poignant in the way Mum, in later years, emphasised to me how much Mr Dent had liked and respected Dad, as if to reassure me. After that meeting, 'HD' seemed to adopt an especially kind and thoughtful attitude towards me. It was as if he were now aware of some unusual need in me: as if he had solved some puzzle that he had been turning over in his mind ever since he began to teach me a year or so earlier. The decision that he and Dad took together was in favour of Greek, and it proved an inspired choice.

For his Christmas present that year Dad bought me a stainless steel wristwatch from J. W. Benson of Bond Street. I am wearing it now; it keeps true time. It was from Benson's that Dad had bought his half-hunter watch when he and Mum were on honeymoon.

The months passed. I slaved at my books. Dad and Mum gave me gentle encouragement and support.

Of course, I now know that many parents will do almost anything for their children, going the extra mile, turning the other cheek, giving them the clothing from their back, going out to meet the returning Prodigal. Yet there is something heart-rending in the way Dad, and along with him Mum, yielded up everything for us. Dad's internal resources were diminishing, and at an accelerating rate. Time was against all four of us, but they saw through to the end faithfully and successfully what they had begun.

※

One sunny Saturday afternoon in 1958 or 1959 Mum's brother, Uncle George called on us. It had never happened before. It meant something. Even at the time I could sense that. I felt frightened.

Uncle George was wearing his best three-piece dark suit. He still made his living from the fruit and vegetable stall in the covered market in Plymouth, which Uncle Arthur had arranged for him in the 1930s. In this way, Arthur had managed to rescue his brother from working at the china clay works at Lee Moor, which was damaging his health.

Uncle Arthur's plan to give George a steady job and a reliable way of earning his living had worked out, although there was the occasional crisis caused by George's gambling and intermittent drinking, combined with his over-generosity when he won 'on the horses'. Once, as Uncle Arthur slipped him half a crown to bale him out of some debt in the 1930s, he said, 'Here it is, waster.'

Dad's account book shows that, from time to time, he lent or gave George small sums of money to help him out, but by that day in 1958 or 1959 it was no longer possible or perhaps wise for him to do so. Dad was already hard pressed by his illness and his care for us. Now he had to summon up the resources to refuse George his request for a loan, much bigger than in the past. Probably George's younger brother Wally had already refused him.

Dad and George discussed this on good terms, and George left cheerfully enough, but I find it difficult to comprehend or, in my heart, even now to forgive his shade for what he put Dad through. But then I remember how many people forgave George so much because of his frank and open nature. In the nursing home where his life drew to its end, Mum visited him faithfully, and she saw how the nurses and other staff warmed to him because of his kindliness and generous spirit. George knew himself and his faults.

Perhaps I also feel that Mum should have told her brother that his behaviour was unacceptable, but probably it had to come from Dad, even if Mum had an inkling of what to expect from George. Somehow George found the money to get by. He always did.

This incident had a big impact on me at the time, although Dad and Mum never mentioned it again in my hearing. It was the cost which, even then, I felt that it exacted from Dad that made it so painful; and the sense it gave me that our life was so fragile.

Ten or eleven years earlier, at Venton, it had been Dad who gave me his hand to hold and steadied me as we walked together up the lane from the well to Saugor Cottage. The comforting grip that had kept me safe was now unsure and weakening, and Dad and I could do nothing about it.

A year later, during the summer holidays, I came in from a cycle ride. I remember going to the front bedroom upstairs to look at the sunset. Dad was lying on the bed, listening to the Henry Wood promenade concert on the radio. In a flash I saw that he had an inner life of his own, a love of music, a need for peace and quiet and restoration. For some reason, I had a hollow sense within me, a fearful, inexplicable feeling that he was slipping away to a distance that could not be bridged.

I loved him so much and still do.

※

In the late 1950s and early 1960s we usually had four weeks' holiday at the caravan. Dad would be with us for two or three weeks; then he would return home to work at Coypool.

On his days off he used to travel out by bus to Bigbury-on-Sea to stay with us. We would walk over the cliffs from Challaborough to meet him at the bus stop. Sometimes I went there in the evening to meet him on my own. Dad and I would walk back to the caravan, cosy and warm, lit softly by its Calor gas lamps. Mum would make us cocoa when we arrived.

That walk with Dad used to make me happy, in the old way. The beam of light from our chrome-plated torch would pick out moths rising from the tall tufts of grass along the sandy footpath, and Dad and I would talk, and I would experience his care and concern for me, his interest in what I was doing and learning. He was quiet and withdrawn by now, but, on our own like that, I felt as I had when we were walking up the hill at Venton together. Even on holiday I studied endlessly, as a refuge from what was happening. Those walks together were a release from the need to escape. Through being alone with him, concentrating just on him, with nothing to distract either of us, and in the dusk we found peace together. As Dad's capacities weakened, Mum's instinct was to seek to fill the gap, the silences. It was rare that Dad and I were alone together and I was able really to be in touch with him.

They both did the best they could, but Huntington's had the whip-hand over us all.

In 1960 I bought a colour film for my Kodak box camera, of which I was very proud. In one photograph, taken by my brother, Mum and I are shown together on the cliff path to Bigbury, accompanying Dad to catch the bus back to work after a couple of days with us. In Dad's face, I see the worry and the anxiety of the situation; in Mum's, the urgency to smile and to make things as well as they could be. My face is a mask.

※

One night, late in the autumn of 1961, I awoke with a start. There was a brief clattering sound and some muffled words.

Tired by the routine of the daily journeys to and from school and by all my study, I sank back into sleep. Outside our bedrooms on the landing, Dad had mistaken his direction and stumbled on his way back to bed from the lavatory. He had fallen down the stairs – all eighteen of them. It may have been a sign that his Huntington's was on the move. It was a decisive moment, and after the fall Dad's health deteriorated more quickly.

Cousin Barbara visited us at this time, soon after her marriage. She noticed Dad's condition with alarm.

For the first time in ten years Mum was ill, with varicose ulcers, brought on, I am sure, by what was happening to Dad. Apart from our caravan holidays (we all felt safe there), there were no more outings or activities for us as a family.

Just before we went to Challaborough in July 1962, Dad made his Will.

※

There could be no escape. We all did our best.

25
'I love you, my darling'

DAD RETIRED at the end of March 1963.

It had been the hardest winter since 1947. Spring came late that year. Even in Devon the ground was hard with frost until the equinox.

The commanding officer at Coypool wrote Dad a farewell letter, thanking him for his loyal, good work for twelve years. He mentioned, with special gratitude, that Dad made his way to work every day, and night, that winter, often walking the two miles there and the two miles back through the snow.

Dad's colleagues were sorry to lose him. They visited him at home at number 10 one afternoon and presented him with a Parker fountain pen which had a stainless steel case. It was a modern version of the one that he had used for so long.

With Mum's support and guidance, Dad established a new routine. Each morning, he would take the wicker shopping-basket (I have it still) and, carrying it over the crook of his left arm, go to Ridgeway to do the shopping, with a list prepared by Mum.

Usually he went first to Mr and Mrs Kelly's grocery shop. Then he would cross the road to visit Mr Vibert at the butcher's shop, and pass Mrs Hawkins' ladies' outfitters where Mum bought her clothes. He would collect the newspaper at Muldowney's stationery shop.

These outings each morning, on his own, were important for Dad. Although some of the shopkeepers sometimes worried that, without Mum's steadying arm, he might fall over, that happened only once or twice in all those years, towards the end when his choreic movements were much more sudden and jerky.

Mum knew how important it was for Dad to go out alone and do this shopping. Once, for a moment revealing their sadness (it hardly ever happened), she told me how much it hurt Dad that 'he could do so little'.

At home, Dad would bring in the coal for the fire in the sitting-room and for the Rayburn, and he would do the dusting. I see him now dusting the stairs, kneeling on each of them as he worked his way down to the hall. He was able to continue to cut the grass for a while.

In December 1963 I won a scholarship to Exeter College, Oxford. Mum and Dad were bursting with pride, they told me. In the early summer of 1964 they took me to Dingle's department store to fit me out. They bought a wonderful aluminium-lined trunk, two sports jackets (this was a time when students still wore middle aged clothes), two pairs of trousers, a tea-set, tea towels, a dressing-gown (I still wear it sometimes) and a small portable radio (an Ekco, like our television set). How did they afford it? I had worked as a deliveryman for the South Western Electricity Board after I left school, but my wages did not pay for all these treasures.

Then came a beautiful September, and we basked in the sun. It was the sunniest and driest September in Devon that century.

And then I was gone. The train pulled slowly up Hemerdon bank, the steepest stretch of mainline track on the old Great Western Railway. I passed the wood known as 'the Plantation', where Dad and Mum waved to me, and looked out at Stuggy Lane where, so often, we had walked together, the four of us.

※

My brother became lonely. Mum and Dad bought him a golden Labrador, 'Rusty'. He became their companion on their daily walks. They had a long walk every day.

After Dad had done his shopping, he and Mum would set out with Rusty up the long hill that rises gently to the east, the continuation of Ridgeway, as far as the drive of Chaddlewood House. In those years there were open fields and a herd of dairy cows. The house is now surrounded by an immense housing estate, a dormitory for Plymouth, built in the late 1970s and 1980s.

On other days, they would walk northwards, beyond Torridge and 'the Plantation' and under the railway bridge to Newnham House.

Then, on their return, they would sit down at the pine table in the kitchen for the stew that they had left cooking slowly in the Rayburn. We called it 'peasant food'. Later, they would enjoy afternoon tea by the fire in the sitting-room.

On Sundays, there was church, St Mary's, where they had been married. Because of his choreic movements, Dad was embarrassed about receiving the Holy Communion. For this reason he had ceased attending the early 8 o'clock service by the mid-1950s. So their service was Evensong. In the university vacation we sometimes joined them in their pew, half-hidden beside one of the granite columns in the north aisle.

Who can tell, but I have the strong impression that this routine supported them, and for several years gave them the strength and peace and contentment that they needed to keep things going. This sense of Dad and Mum's steady, peaceful routine also saved me. I owe them everything.

Two years later my brother joined me at Oxford.

Our parents' routine became less easy as Dad's condition worsened. In the spring of 1966, I cancelled a trip to Greece to visit the archaeological sites because of my anxiety about Dad.

A year later I received a travel scholarship from my College. I hesitated. My ancient history tutor, Dacre Balsdon, asked me, not unkindly but in ignorance, 'Can't someone else look after your parents while you are away?' I doubted it and did not know how to reply, but with two friends from the College I made the trip and spent five weeks there.

Only recently have I learnt that my tutor's sympathy may have owed something to the loss he suffered of his own father just before he went up to Oxford in 1920. He remained a bachelor. In his early years as a tutor his responsibilities for his mother and two younger brothers and a sister prevented his marrying the young woman with whom he fell in love. Dacre never spoke of this sadness; his family told me of it many years later.

On my return from Greece, Dad's condition shocked me. It seemed so much worse, but I had to return to Oxford a few days later.

There was a crisis soon after my brother and I left. Mum had to make a visit to the doctor's surgery. Dr Owen's note records that she was suffering from anxiety and loss of appetite. He also wrote, 'her husband is in hospital'. Of this Mum and Dad told us nothing.

By the time we returned to number 10 in June for the long vacation, their old routine had been restored and Dad's short stay in Moorhaven Hospital seemed to have stabilised the situation.

That summer, and after I graduated in 1968, we had many happy afternoons together, with picnics by a remote stream at a place that we called Lane End, on the edge of Dartmoor. My car made this possible. It was a Morris Minor 1000, PCO 293. I had bought it in April 1966 when I finished the first part of my degree. For the purpose I used the expired National Savings Certificates that Dad had bought for me many years earlier. That rather odd decision proved to be one of the best I ever made. That Morris gave us pure joy at a time when we needed it.

In October that year I went to Cambridge to read for a further degree. The following Christmas was not easy for any of us. Then, in late February 1969, I came home again for a few days.

Immediately, I realised that the game was up. The pressure on Mum was unbearable. I still have nightmares about Cambridge, and find it an agony to go there.

In the middle of one night, when I got up to go to the lavatory, the light was burning on the landing. There was a note in Mum's handwriting lying on the rug just outside my door. It was written in biro on a piece of cardboard from a skein of the wool that Mum used for darning our socks. The note said (I still have it),

'John, we leave the light on overnight on the landing,' a safety precaution for Dad and their peace of mind.

The next day, the twenty-sixth, I called on Dr Owen to talk to him about the situation. In his dry but kindly way, he expressed his concern. I asked him if the condition was 'congenital'. 'I'm sorry to have to tell you that it is hereditary,' he said.

I stumbled out of the surgery. On the doorstep there I knew beyond any doubt that one day I must write this book. God spoke to me.

I walked to Coypool at Marsh Mills where Dad had worked so long and called on Jessie, Mum and Dad's old friend who had worked in the doctors' surgery for years. Jessie gave me a cup of coffee. She told me that she knew of Dad's affliction. 'Is it Huntington's chorea?' she said. We talked. She was very kind.

Afterwards, I walked up the old railway track to Plymbridge. In my confusion, I knew that my life was changed at a stroke. I walked home.

Later that day I told Mum, in the kitchen, that Dr Owen had explained the situation to me. Mum looked worried. We agreed that, as soon as his exams were safely written in reasonable peace of mind in June, she should tell my brother about it. She did so, the most terrible thing imaginable for her.

Back in Cambridge, I decided immediately to terminate my course. I applied for jobs and joined the Civil Service. I started work in the Treasury in October 1969. I was determined to earn my living and, if possible, to make some contribution to my parents. By the skin of our teeth, we made it.[5]

---

5 When I joined the Treasury my only black, office shoes let in the rain, and my office suit was threadbare.

In August that year, while I was still in Cambridge, Dad had to be admitted to Moorhaven as a permanent patient. He was able to return home to number 10 only once, for Christmas the following year. Margaret Pearce, another daughter of Mum's old friend at the hardware shop in Ridgeway, lent me her mini van, and I was able to collect and return Dad safely. It was a beautiful day, frosty and sunny. We all enjoyed it.

For three years Dad lived as a patient at the hospital. The staff liked him; they respected him. They saw something of what he really was. Mum visited him three times a week, travelling on the special bus from Plymouth to the hospital at Bittaford, twelve miles east of Plympton. Often she visited him every day. Somehow, she found time to bake buns for him, sometimes enough for all the patients in his ward. When I was able to get down from work in London I used to hire a car and take Dad and Mum for a drive. We used to go to Lane End, with its many happy memories.

As Dad settled in at the hospital, he became more stable. His weight went up to 9st 6lb, and his face filled out and had a good colour. He used to help Mum do the Daily Telegraph cryptic crossword. Once she wrote to me, 'I was doing the crossword on Wednesday and didn't know how to spell "trigonometry", and Dad knew! I asked him and he spelt it immediately. I was so pleased. His brain is very active.'

In March 1971 Judy and I got engaged. Mum wrote to me, 'I gently explained to Dad about you and Judy and he seemed pleased, and agreed that it would be lovely for you to be happily married. I wish with all my heart that he were well enough to see the wedding; still, we have to be thankful that he is content, warm and comfortable. The nurse told me that they all think a great deal of him as he is so gentle.'

Five months later Judy and I were married. I owe her as much as I owe Mum and Dad. She is very brave. It is her great regret that she never knew Dad. We have now known each other fifty three years, thank God.

Mum wrote to us as we settled into our first house, at Ely, 'It was a lovely, happy wedding and we all enjoyed it ... Judy looked beautiful ... A day to remember.'

She added, 'At the hospital, they told me that Dad was kicking a ball on the lawn while you and Judy were being married. It was telepathy. We were happy and it was transported to him! I couldn't believe it, but the nice male nurse said it was so.'

It happened just that once.

In the early months of 1972, a chest and stomach infection went around the ward three times. Mum told me, 'It has made Dad very poorly ... He sends his love. He always eats the egg custard that I bake for him, I'm glad to say.'

In May 1972 Mum wrote to me, 'I go to the hospital every day as Dad is very poorly with this infection. Yesterday I took the colour snaps of Challaborough ... He seemed interested ... He is in bed until the infection clears up ... I go to Loughtor Mill every evening with Rusty and it tires me pleasantly for my night's rest.'

Dad rallied a little, but became very thin. At the beginning of June Mum wrote, 'Dad had a temperature yesterday and I had to give him a lot to drink ... I now know what he means by "Help me", and I get the nurse to turn him. He is very thin, but the nurse said he is eating his meals and he drinks the milky coffee that I take him ... Sometimes I take a little bit of strawberry, caster sugar and cream, about four strawberries mashed up, and he eats this.'

At the end of the month Mum told me, 'Dad is as comfortable as they can make him on the ripple bed, and the charge nurse says that he is such a good patient and never complains. The nurses are gentle and kind, and Dr Lilanwala is wonderful ... They are really doing all they can.'

In mid-July, Dad developed a further chest infection, which turned to pneumonia. My brother and I borrowed a friend's blue MG and raced down to the hospital from Ely, where Judy and I had made our first home.

That afternoon Dad said clearly to Mum, 'I love you, my darling,' his last words.

Just before we arrived, as Mum was feeding him, Dad choked and lost his breath. It was a quick end. We kissed him on the forehead. He still had thick, white hair, neatly trimmed.

We drove down the steep lane, so like the hill at Venton where I have my first memory of Dad, and then made our way together, the three of us, home to number 10.

26
'... down to Oxford's towers'

EARLY IN THE EVENING of a day in late July 1972, soon after Dad's funeral, I parked the blue MG Midget carefully at the side of the quiet road that runs along the ridge of Boar's Hill to the south of Oxford. There was no other car in sight. Mum and I struggled out of the low leather seats. We crossed the road and leant on a five-bar gate.

We gazed down at Oxford far beyond the fields in which black and white Friesian cattle grazed. The air was clear. With Dad's binoculars, brought back from India, we could pick out the towers and spires of churches and colleges, even the graceful curves of the Sheldonian Theatre and the Radcliffe Camera, golden in the sunset.

Mum soaked in the view. It was the first time that she had glimpsed what, at such cost to them, she and Dad had enabled my brother and me to enjoy.

Dad never saw that view.

Mum and I drove down into Oxford, over the River Isis and up St Aldate's. The streets were empty. It was as if the High and the Broad, Magdalen Bridge and St Giles, the whole of Oxford, had reserved these few minutes for Mum alone, to take in all its beauty and grace, chaste and pure of every other person and impression.

Knowing that this experience would never be repeated, I drove back to Boar's Hill. Again, we stood at the gate and fed on what we saw in the distance.

'I can't go on,' Mum said. She was suddenly weighed down by the harsh contrast between the glory before us and the loss of Dad after their twenty-eight years together, so many of them dominated by Huntington's.

'You've got to go on,' I said. 'If you give up, we're finished.'

Mum knew that it was true. She formed an iron will and never yielded.

We turned away from Boar's Hill and Oxford. We made our way to Ely. Judy had already returned there after Dad's funeral, and she was waiting to welcome Mum on her first visit to stay with us for a few days.

Mum and I never again spoke to each other of our conversation on Boar's Hill. We never told anyone else of it. She treasured Dad in her heart, and between the two of them, she and Dad, and the resolution that she formed on Boar's Hill, saved us all.

27
'Dearly loved husband, father and brother'

IT TOOK YEARS to take it all in.

It is difficult to remember the few months that followed Dad's death. Everything else is so clear in my memory. Once or twice, I believe, I went on the bus to Moorhaven Hospital. I wanted to recall how it had been in those last three years of Dad's life there.

In those three years the bus used to drop me at Bittaford, and I would slowly climb the hill, one-in-seven, or even one-in-five, under the railway viaduct. With me I would have the old brown plastic bucket-bag that I had used for so many years at the caravan, when I used to pack it with a towel and swimming trunks, and, later, with Homer's *Iliad* or *Odyssey* to read on the beach after a swim. When I had been visiting Dad in hospital, the bag had held a thermos of tea and two peaches. Peaches were soft, safe for me to peal and cut slices to give Dad, with no risk of his choking. His ability to swallow was affected by then.

I slip in through the heavy iron gates at the hospital lodge and walk up the long drive and through the grand, airy entrance hall. For the most part, the building is quiet, the atmosphere peaceful. The passages seem as long as the drive outside, and the rubbery linoleum deadens the sound as I walk. Wards open off the corridor every so often. Then, in the distance, I catch sight of Dad: a dark Cornish complexion, just over six feet tall, still with his slim build, but afflicted by a lurching, unsteady gait, shrugging his shoulders, eyes opening wider than is natural, head lolling a little to right or left from time to time.

Only in sleep is Dad at rest. Occasionally I see him like that, as I sit beside him in the ward.

Everyone in the ward likes Dad. They try to make things as nice as possible for him.

The notice of Dad's death that Mum had put in the newspaper testifies to this:

> SYMONS: On July 22, after a long illness, including three years' devoted care at Moorhaven Hospital, Major William John Symons, MBE, IA (Retired), of Plympton, Devon, dearly beloved husband, father and brother. Funeral at Plympton St Mary's, two pm, July 26. Donations, if desired, to League of Friends of Moorhaven Hospital, Ivybridge, Devon.

※

Another way that I tried to make sense of it all, in those days just after Dad died, was to go over the short talks we had been able to have, even in the last months at home. There was one that I often thought about. It would be easy to misunderstand it, yet in a way it expresses the most important thing about him. Without this, nothing makes sense. It is this that made it possible for him to live the life he lived.

Dad was wearing his dressing gown, blue and grey, with a blue cord. It was the early summer of 1969, when Dad was as ill as it was possible to be without being admitted into care at Moorhaven. In those last months at home, he could not always get properly dressed, for all Mum's efforts, and his, to keep life as normal as possible for us.

So while Mum is shopping in Ridgeway, I am sitting with Dad in the dining-room. I try to divert him by reading him something from *The Forsyte Saga*, which he and Mum have recently watched on the television, but it does not help. Dad cannot concentrate; he cannot keep calm.

A few months ago Dad stopped reading. His glasses and the book, his last book, *Far From the Madding Crowd*, with a makeshift bookmark slipped in at the page where he stopped, are placed on the mantelpiece. This book and Dad's reading-glasses, in their worn, mottled, grey case, will stay there until we sell the house thirty one years later. One part of Dad's life died when he stopped reading. There were so many stations marking the way like that.

So, Dad is standing in the dining-room beside his old armchair. He is swaying a little, from side to side, to and fro; he lifts one leg or the other, and flexes his knees. He hunches up his shoulders and shrugs. Then, for a moment, he is at rest and his mind is clear. He knows that he is with me; his voice is steady and calm. He looks me in the eye and says, 'Before this I trusted God completely.' The moment of peace passes. It seemed that the world had stood still. Dad is all unwilled movement again.

Dad's words hit me in the heart and crush the breath

out of me. My eyes sting and my spine tingles. I just sit there, gingerly on the edge of the second armchair, the one that Dad cannot use any more.

A few weeks ago his body and limb movements were so fierce that he was thrown sideways; he fell from the chair, and the force that was whipping through his body broke one of its back legs. I mended it in a rough and ready way, screwing it together. We cannot throw the chair away. Money is short now.

'Before this I trusted God completely.'

And I know that it is true. Dad is true, through and through.

But the question that hits me in a second wave, and makes my eyes sting again, is this. Was it all in vain?

This trust, this faith was growing in him from the first. It was handed down by his grandparents and his parents. And this faith, this attitude, is there already in Dad's hand as it rests lightly on his mother's left shoulder in the family photograph taken just after her husband's death. It is there, in the way the seven children regularly went to church and chapel, Sunday by Sunday. It is there, in the firm writing in the prayer and hymn book with which Dad was issued or which he bought in India: '5430269 Pte. J. Symons. A/Coy 1/DCLI, Lucknow, India, 9 November 1924'; in the Family Bible that he bought later: 'J Symons. Sgt. May 12, 1934'; and, in a finer, educated hand, in a combined Book of Common Prayer and Hymns Ancient and Modern: 'J Symons. Saugor, CP. January 20th 1940.'

It is there, in the Prayer Book, in the underlining that he made in his favourite psalms and hymns. There is an especially emphatic marking beside hymn 176:

> How sweet the name of JESUS sounds
> In a believer's ear!
> It soothes his sorrows, heals his wounds
> And drives away his fears.

Above the hymn is printed a quotation from the New Testament: 'unto you therefore which believe He is precious'.

Was it all in vain?

What I saw and heard and felt in those times was as bad as anything I have ever known. A distinguished consultant neurologist in London later told me that he regarded it as the worst illness that he knew. Of course, it affected my own hopes for a healthy life and more besides, but at that time such thoughts about myself did not come to me. It was what I saw in Dad alone that found every target in me.

And there is one parallel that I know of which helps me understand this. It is when, at the end of all things – or so it seemed – Jesus, tortured and nailed to the Cross, calls to his Father: 'My God, My God, why hast Thou forsaken me?'

He utters a loud cry: 'It is all completed,' and He dies. He is finished.

When Jesus uttered His cry of dereliction, of abandonment, was He asking, 'What have I done, God, to cause you to abandon me?' Or was he asking, 'To what purpose have You abandoned me?'

No, it was not the first. For Jesus did not believe that His Heavenly Father rewarded sin with disaster, or goodness with success. His Father makes the sun to shine and the rain to fall equally on the just and the unjust. When a crowd surrounding Jesus were complaining about His interest in a crippled man who had probably, they said, brought his misfortune on himself, Jesus healed him. The purpose of the affliction was that He might show God's mercy and healing. So, in his cry of dereliction, Jesus was perhaps asking about the purpose of God in his Passion.

For his part, Dad did not ask, in my hearing, 'Why me?' There is no answer to that. Huntington's just happens, like so many other things to so many people.

But that Dad's suffering had a meaning and purpose, I am clear. Its meaning was the way he and Mum behaved; in their goodness they revealed God's goodness. They kept their eyes on that and somehow found a meaning in it all. With that faith, and for the sake of their children, they could endure all things.

In my heart I know only one way to understand what happened to Dad. I remember all that he had done and achieved against terrible odds; the integrity with which he had done it; the way he saw through to the bitter end what he undertook – loving us to the uttermost, even when, at moments, I regarded him as living yet dead.

For this is what Dad means to me, the manner in which he continued to live for us for twenty years after the worst began to happen:

> Take to heart what you found in Christ Jesus.
> He was in the form of God,
> yet He reckoned that no reason for grasping for Himself,
> but made Himself nothing,
> taking the form of a slave.
> Bearing human likeness, sharing the human lot,
> He humbled himself, and was obedient, even to death,
> death on a cross.
> Therefore God raised Him to the heights

and bestowed on Him the name above all names ...
to the glory of God the Father.'

> St Paul, Epistle to the Philippians, Ch 2, v 5-11

Dad did, indeed, take that message to heart. What Dad did, how he lived as one of Jesus' followers, mirrored Jesus' way. And Dad's death, like that of the One Whom he followed, was not the end.

28
A New Life

AFTER HER RETURN to number 10 from Ely, Mum began to build a new life. It took time.

For years taking care of Dad had been the centre of everything. And, for all the problems and sadness, they had still found happiness together. Running number 10, telephone calls in the evening to Wally, and visits from Hilda and Fred – all this had seen them through the last years of Dad's illness. Their walks and good meals kept them fit.

Mum's new life would last twenty-three years at home and then nearly three in hospital.

There were two setbacks in the first couple of years. Hilda died of pneumonia in January 1973, leaving Fred a widower. At the end of October 1974, Rusty died.

Each of them left a big gap.

Step by step Mum created a new routine that gave her life shape and purpose.

Each day began early. Before she got dressed, she prayed at her bedside. Then she opened the front door to bring in the milk-bottle from the doorstep and greeted the light with the words, 'The Glory of the Lord', and 'I will lift up mine eyes unto the hills from whence cometh my help, even from the Lord' as she looked over the village towards Dorsmouth Rock, the hill between Plympton and Saltram.

Mum had a good breakfast beside the Rayburn.

After breakfast she read her Bible. It is heavily worn. Her favourite passage in the New Testament – the page is threadbare and stained from her constant reference to it – was from the first letter of St Peter, chapter one:

> Blessed be the God and Father of our Lord Jesus Christ. Through His great mercy we are born again to a living hope through the resurrection of Christ Jesus from the dead.

On a piece of paper, now dog-eared and much repaired, among the prayers that she used every day, she had written these words:

> O Lord, the God of all strength,
> We pray that you will comfort and help all who are in trouble, sickness or distress.
> Reveal yourself to them that they may know your peace,
> Through Jesus Christ, Our Lord. Amen.

Between the pages of her Bible is a text which she cut from the personal column of the newspaper one day and on which she used to meditate:

> I wish above all things that thou mayest prosper and be in health, even as thy soul prospereth.
> (3 John, verse 2)

Mum prayed unceasingly that we might be spared Huntington's chorea. In her diary, at one difficult period, she wrote: 'I am sorry to have brought such sadness to my family.' In fact, she and Dad were utterly innocent: they could not have understood the situation in the 1940s.

She would have preferred to be at risk herself, rather than the two of us. She wished that this were possible with force and sincerity, as great a sacrifice as one person can offer for another, as if she gave up her own life repeatedly for us, day by day.

Alongside her faith, Mum's stubbornness and simplicity sustained her. She could be shrewd and wise, take a long view of disasters and see them turning into successes, endure all manner of sorrows and yet take joy in life. She could always tap into the deepest wells of her heart, the heart of the child who had made darts from pins, corks and chicken feathers; who had identified with 'Jakey', the patient donkey, pulling the trap with the children to a Sunday school outing at the beach at Wembury; who had made marmalade from orange peel in a tin can over a fire in the back-garden. Mum delighted in things that cost little or nothing.

Almost as soon as Mum had washed up the dishes, Fred used to call on her for coffee and cheese and biscuits. On his way to or from work at the police station my cousin Jack often dropped in to see that all was well and stayed for a while.

After the Second World War, Fred had settled down as a driver for the Electricity Board. He had become utterly reliable and steady, a man of good humour and gentle kindness.

In their many years as widower and widow, Fred and Mum were the best of friends. She used to remind him occasionally that at his wedding the vicar had enjoined him to take good care of Hilda with the words, 'Do not let this beautiful flower fade.' The Vicar had noticed, with some alarm, that Fred had arrived for the service wearing two left boots.

Fred took all the old stories from Mum in good part. The horror of all that he had seen in the Army when he was present at the opening of the concentration camp at Belsen sometimes took its toll on his nerves, but after a few days in hospital he again became stoical, generous, mild and full of sympathetic humour, a very present help in trouble to Mum and others. They were faithful friends.

Fred was as fond of the elevenses with Mum as she was pleased to see him. If the weather was kind, they would go into the garden to see what was growing. They used to count the flowers on the clematis and the roses.

The gardens, front and back, grew more and more important to Mum as each of the twenty-three years after Dad's death passed. The back garden was overgrown but beautiful and peaceful.

In the garden at the front of the house Mum and Dad had inherited or planted viburnum fragrans, daphne odora and daphne mezereum, a miniature Japanese lilac, chaenomales (japonica), a white azalea which, every May, produced an expanse of white flowers ('like an angel's wings,' Mum said), a viburnum bodnantense with an intoxicating scent, forsythia, a carpet of bluebells, wallflowers, and kaffir lilies (schistostyles). Beside the front gate there was a tiny rose bush which had been there since Victorian times, perhaps put there by number 10's first owners. This rose produced a flower, its first for some years, and then died, in the year of Mum's death.

After an hour or so with Mum, Fred went for a pint of beer and something to eat with his friends at the Constitutional Club in Ridgeway.

On most days Mum cooked her 'peasant food' for lunch. She listened to the 'Afternoon Theatre' play on Radio 4 at the kitchen table. As her hearing worsened and listening to the radio became more difficult, she began to watch films on the television in the afternoon. Once when she was telling me about all the films that she had enjoyed by the fire, she said, 'One does not get old without getting artful.'

Mum built her life on routine; she contemplated life, and the world, and the beyond. This made life possible for her. 'Having a fire; doing some weeding when you feel like it; doing the crossword by the fire – it all helps,' she said to me.

Sometimes she found it difficult to get going with her house-work. 'I've been reading St. Paul's letters to the Thessalonians and this morning's piece says, "If anyone will not work, let him not eat." So I think I'd better get on with some work.'

The evenings were tedious in winter, but in summer Mum enjoyed the sunsets through her sitting-room window – golden, opal, aquamarine. As the evening star began to shine, she put out her empty milk bottle, brightly polished, on the front doorstep for the milkman to collect the next morning. She looked across Moorland Road to number 3, near the turning into Ridgeway, to check that the light was shining in Mrs Wyndham Hull's bedroom, showing that she was safe. Every night Mrs Wyndham Hull did the same for Mum.

※

Peggy, Judy's mother, did a lot to help Mum.

She had lost her husband, Noel, eighteen months

before Dad died. The two of them often spoke on the telephone, with Peggy reporting to Mum on the trips she made to stay with us. Mum loved to hear this news. She was touched by the way that Peggy helped her face the loss of Dad. She often spoke to me about this.

In the early spring of 1973, soon after Hilda's death, Peggy first drove over from her home near Ottery St Mary in East Devon to visit Mum. She stayed a night.

Mum had already taken Judy to her heart. In a letter to her at this time she wrote, 'Did I ever tell you that you are a comfort to me, Judy?'

She never met Noel but she had heard of his kindness as Vicar of Wembury. 'There is a lady I ride with on the bus to Moorhaven who comes from Wembury. She told me that Judy's father was a wonderful clergyman and went to see everyone, no matter whether they were church or chapel or didn't go anywhere at all. She was sad to hear that he had died.'

Peggy's visit went well.

> I took Peggy her early morning tea in bed when she stayed with me and her pretty face came up from under the bedclothes...
>
> We went for a walk through the pathfields to St Maurice and sat on the top of the castle mound for a long time in the sunshine, looking at the view over Plympton, the cottages and the lawn at the bottom where children were playing...
>
> Peggy enjoyed the roast beef that I cooked for her...
> It is easy to like Peggy.

After the visit Peggy wrote to me:

> I thoroughly enjoyed being with your mother and she was very good to me. She sat on my bed while we

> drank our early morning tea... I'm so glad that she is going away to Scotland with your brother. It will give her lots to think about for a long time afterwards... The house was beautifully warm! I've just had a visit from the Samaritan leader from Exeter and I hope to join them if I'm approved.

Peggy stayed with Mum a second time eighteen months later.

> I had a little chat with Peggy on the phone yesterday. I rang to congratulate her on her son's wedding and to wish them all health and happiness... On Thursday Peggy is coming for a day and night!

Peggy took Mum a jar of apple pickle, some dessert apples and a bunch of pinks from her wonderful garden at West Hill in the country between Ottery St Mary and Sidmouth. They had become firm friends and sat by the fire and talked. 'I was sorry when she went. How well she looks,' Mum wrote.

※

In May 1975 we took Mum to visit Peggy. It would be the last time they saw each other.

> I so much enjoyed going to Ottery St Mary and seeing Peggy's new house... I thought that she was looking well and it will be lovely when she is better. It was a day to remember.

In June I had to give Mum the bad news that Peggy's cancer had spread – a possibility that she had probably mentioned to Mum on her last visit to number 10. Later Mum wrote to me:

> I'm feeling very sad about Peggy. Will you and Judy tell me if there is anything I can do? I am very fond of her – she has a lovely nature. Your news is such a shock that my brain is not functioning properly. I have shed a lot of tears this morning.

At the end of August Peggy died. She was the same age as Mum.

Mum was devastated by her death. In her diary, on the day before the funeral, she wrote, 'Today I feel lonely.' The following day she read the full burial service from the Prayer Book at home as the service was being conducted.

> If only she could have had five more years... I'm very glad that I knew her – a lovely person. Each time I go into the entrance to St Maurice pathfields I think of our walk together. It was just after the new road was made and I could not find the entrance. Peggy said, 'Is this the way?' We were both amused that she found it although I have lived here so long.

At St Mary's church on the Sunday after the funeral Mum became upset about Peggy's death. She told me that she 'had to come out of church', midway through the Holy Communion service.

Happy memories of Peggy stayed strong with Mum. Year by year she remembered Peggy's birthday on the sixth of June. 'I thought yesterday of a lovely person whose birthday it would have been.' Later, in hospital she often spoke of Peggy's kindness to her and of her affection for her. She reminded me of a visit she had paid to her in her cottage at West Hill.

> I remember the flowers and butterflies at her cottage. She gave me some lovely soup, and when I told her

that I liked it she said it was 'only out of a tin'... She used to say that if she didn't make a pudding, she'd be happy with bread and marmalade. Sometimes she used to eat it before going to bed.

She was a lovely person, and I got on very well with her.

※

Mum was tempted to have a new dog after Rusty died. Her brother Jack offered her 'a Labrador puppy for my birthday, but I refused as there can be only one dog for me.'

She did not often see Jack, but he used to send her an occasional rabbit or pigeon until his death in 1976. There were many local countrymen at his funeral at St Mary's church, the final generation of a type of Englishman who had, for centuries, lived that sort of rustic life. Mr Matthews, the Vicar, who also enjoyed pigeon or rabbit stew, said in his address that Jack was 'one of the old school who lived close to nature'. Jack had never been registered with a doctor under the National Health Service until the stroke that killed him after three days in hospital.

Soon after that Mum lay awake all night because she had seen a litter of Labrador puppies. 'They are entrancing, but I must be strong and decline. Sadly, I am getting on in years.'

It was the beginning of a long, hard winter.

29
Windwhistle

IN THE 1970s British Rail introduced a new fleet of high-speed trains on the Western Region line from Paddington station to Penzance. These trains made the journey to Plymouth in a little less than three hours at their best, and comfortably in three and a half hours.

There was a wonderful timetable. From time to time I could visit Mum for the day on a Saturday.

At Paddington I went to the front of the train and settled down in a seat next door to the guard's compartment, with my back to the engine. At times the train accelerated suddenly to top speed. Sometimes the driver had to brake sharply, and the pungent, acrid smell of the brakes lingered in the air for a while.

Few people used the 7.25 train in the winter months. It can never have paid its way. In those years that seemed not to matter. I sometimes felt that the train had been laid on especially for me. I strode from one end of it to the other to buy tea or coffee or simply for the exercise as I recovered from my week's work bent over a desk.

In Plymouth I took a taxi and reached number 10 by 11 o'clock. Often Uncle Fred was there, 'ever faithful' in Mum's words, and she gave us coffee by the Rayburn.

Uncle Fred went on his way, and Mum cooked us pasties or roast beef. After that we went for a walk, and then had tea by the fire in the sitting-room. Then I would be off by taxi to catch the 6.35 train, getting home before 11pm.

On one Saturday in early February the sun was unusually warm. Mum and I packed two of her pasties (golden brown and just out of the oven) in a blue tea-cosy decorated with various garden birds. We set off on a long walk. We visited the lanes through which Mum and Dad had walked with us and the old push-chair in the early 1950s.

We walked past the Plantation and up Stuggy Lane, alongside the railway line. We went under the railway bridge, and up the hill, past the 'chimney pot', a pottery chute through which the winter rainwater from the drains under the fields gushed on its way to cascade down the hill. As a little boy I had stood and gazed at this mysterious sight and fished with a hazel stick in the torrential stream.

Mum and I pressed on to West Park Hill. We walked on the footpath through the fields to the village of Hemerdon. Beyond the village we made a seat among the bright yellow celandines on the bank of a high hedge. In the distance we could see the waters of Plymouth Sound and the cliffs of Cornwall.

We set about the pasties, still hot and steaming.

Judy asked Mum for advice about making pasties:

Plain flour, for me, is essential. Self-raising flour soaks up the juice into it. My idea is that onion is very important and I use a medium one in each for juice, and a bit of turnip [swede is called turnip in Devon and

Cornwall] cut small and of course, potato. Just lately I've used skirt. I would never have done so in the past – I always used best steak. So after rolling the pastry and placing the meat, potato, turnip and onion on it, I put a knob of butter or marge on top before closing it all in. No, I don't soak the vegetables, Judy. I bet your pasties turn out lovely!

After an hour there taking in the view from Hemerdon and watching the birds and some horses in a field, Mum and I stirred ourselves. We walked back through Windwhistle Wood and down the lower drive from Newnham House, overgrown with gigantic rhododendrons. After we had had a cup of tea and a slice of her Madeira cake, Mum played Elgar's *Chanson de Matin* and *To Music* by Schubert. The taxi arrived to take me to the railway station. 'I shall not forget today,' Mum wrote; nor would I.

It was on these visits that Mum and I were able most deeply to share our love of Dad and our memories and our faith. Judy's understanding and love made it possible for Mum and me to have those days together.

Occasionally I stayed the Saturday night at number 10. Normally we went to Holy Communion at eight o'clock at St Mary's, but one Sunday we woke up very early and went for a walk instead. There was something about the clear air, the sharp frost, and the sense of the passing years and the changes coming to Plympton that said 'Go now. You may never have this chance again.'

We walked out to the Tory Brook, where a bridge crossed the stream on the way to Torridge. Mum had played there as a child, wriggling her toes in the mud in the summers before the First World War. That morning the edges of the stream were frozen.

We walked on to the Plantation, meeting one of the regular couples setting out for the eight o'clock service. Apart from them, all was still and silent. We stood and watched a pair of bullfinches playing in the hedge, their breasts seeming redder and their rumps whiter than ever in the clear air and bright sunshine. This quiet scene held us in a trance.

At the Plantation we looked up and down the railway line, hoping for a train. Mum recalled how often she and her family had stood there, waving to relatives setting off on some journey. 'We were great wavers,' she said.

We walked back to number 10 for porridge and a boiled egg. Then I was away to London.

30
Neighbours and Friends

ON MIDSUMMER DAY one year Mum wrote to me:

> The weather is superb. I go out early to the shops and then spend the day mooching in the house and watering and admiring the garden. I've been saving water for months; we've had weeks of dry, sunny weather. The 'Star of India' clematis has the most lovely dark, velvety flowers with a red stripe. The 'blue' rose in the back garden is terrific, one mass of parma violet colour, and the hebe is about to flower. The Penelope rose, in the front garden, is falling now after a fantastic show...
>
> I have just been sitting on Mr Pearse's garden seat with him in his front garden for twenty minutes. I left before he told me to go: quite a shock for him!
>
> Saw a marvellous film yesterday afternoon... Shall soon be preparing my peasant food: one onion, a small slice of braising steak, one potato, with lots of cabbage... Then I proceed to the sitting-room to see my film, do two lines of the rug, read dear old *Woman's Weekly*, have tea, water the garden, television, bed...

Sometimes the day did not start so well:

> This morning I got up feeling very grumpy and tired from all the work I have been doing for Mr Short

while Kathleen has been in hospital. The weather is abominable, too.

I was sitting on the arm of the chair in the sitting-room when a red bus went by in Moorland Road. Written on it in big letters were the words 'It's a wonderful world'. Very funny, and that brought me to my senses.

※

Although she saw quite a lot of her immediate neighbours (the Pearses and the Shorts), Mum practised solitude and simplicity. In hospital, dreaming of a return to number 10, which she knew could never take place, she said: 'I want to be plain and ordinary. If you can just be nothing, and get along every day like that, it's much better than being something. Just being quiet: that's lovely, isn't it?'

It was true, but there was more to it. Mum did love quiet and solitude, but she also sometimes relished company. All the old Plymptonians knew her, and so did many of the newcomers. She was popular. Something about her stayed in the mind and affection of those whom she had known or worked with decades earlier.

It was as if she filled a spot in people's hearts or souls that would otherwise have been empty. On one of her rare visits to buy clothes in Plymouth when she was well into her sixties, she called in at Spooner's department store. In the hosiery department Mum approached a counter where the assistant was bent almost double, peering into the bottom drawer of the cabinet and unable to see who was approaching.

'Can you help me with...?' Mum began.

'Of course I can, Grace,' replied the assistant, without looking up from the drawer. It was a one-time colleague of Mum's at Yeo's. They had not seen each other for almost fifty years.

Time was beginning to race.

※

It was meeting the 'eight-o'clockers', the regular worshippers at the early Holy Communion service at St Mary's, that gave Mum her main social gathering each week. Sunday by Sunday her diary records:

'8 o'clock Communion,' and '6.30 Evensong.'

It is sad to read week by week, in her last years at home, 'No Holy Communion,' as she began to suffer more often from varicose ulcers on her legs. She struggled hard to get there into her eighties.

Mum must often have been lonely, despite the comfort of the routine that she built. She rarely told us about it. She never asked anything of us. She knew that we came to visit her as often as we could. She believed that often a trouble shared is a trouble passed to another. In her diaries, for all their brief entries, there are hints of days when her solitude became loneliness.

Years later she would tell me something that related to it as a joke. Sometimes, after we had left number 10 to go back to London, Mum sat at the kitchen table and 'howled'.

Through the party wall Mrs Short, in number 12, heard Mum wailing. She went in to see her for a cup of tea, taking with her, perhaps, a slice of the wonderful Victoria sponge that she used to bake, spread through with blackberry jam made from the brambles growing on her back garden wall. Kathleen had suffered from diabetes since her youth and could not eat the cakes that she made for Gordon, her cantankerous, truculent but well-meaning husband.

Once, the sadness of Dad's illness and death, and her sense of loss at the end of our visit, overwhelmed Mum. She wailed to Mrs Short, 'Kathleen, I wasn't good enough for Jack.'

Understanding Mum through and through, she replied, 'Of course you weren't good enough for him, Grace. We all know that.' With these words Kathleen rescued Mum from despair.

To the end of her life the words, 'Of course you weren't, Grace,' gave Mum comfort. They always triggered her laughter.

Gordon had worked as a tailor and as a commercial traveller in his time, taking goods to the small farms of south Devon. He was an awkward customer. 'Poor Kathleen,' Mum used to say.

Sometimes Gordon would meet someone coming to visit Mum on the doorstep. 'Go in there and you'll find Grace sitting down,' Mr Short used to say to them, much to Mum's disgust. He could not come to terms with Mum's quietist nature, but it was her contemplative attitude that enabled Mum to cope with what she had to endure, to relish all the joys she found, and contentedly to live a life that others would have found lonely.

Gordon had a strong streak of kindness. He was easily moved to sympathy and genuine tears by the suffering of others. Both he and Kathleen were sincere Methodists. Their only child had died of measles when very young.

Gordon owned a pianola. For years he delighted in pretending to Mum and everyone else that he was an accomplished pianist. One lady commented to Mum, 'I can forgive Mr Short anything for being such a musician.'

Gordon saw the joke. He knew his faults, and that was endearing.

※

Mum's neighbours at number 8, Walter and Nancy Pearse, became a source of comfort and helped her face her new life. The three of them became good friends.

Walter served in the First World War. He was seriously injured in the last months of hostilities. In the 1920s, back from the Great War, he began to court Nancy, taking her to tennis parties at houses around Plympton. When he and Mum became friends, although she remained in awe of him, she told him how good-looking he had been in those days. He was 'dashing', she said, dressed in his tennis whites.

> He and his brother, Frank, were so handsome when I was young. They used to drive around the village in Walter's green sports car.

Walter was a man of deep, kindly feelings, and was perhaps more moved by sentiment than he realised. Although they were well off, he and Nancy always stayed on in the terraced house where they had made their home in 1929. The terrace had the best position in the village, he said, on fairly high ground, looking west down a gentle slope towards the afternoon and evening sun. There were glorious sunsets, reflecting the light on the sea four or five miles away.

Walter and Nancy were occasional churchgoers at St Mary's. In hospital, Mum said to me, 'I can see him now, in his tweed suit, with a sprig of daphne odora in his buttonhole, going off to church with Nancy on Easter Sunday.'

Nancy's last years were difficult. She became disabled by arthritis, and suffered a poor hip replacement operation. 'I had a long chat with Mr Pearse... He and Mrs Pearse are fed up because she is very closed in and cannot walk. He was glad to have a talk. The Pearses are dears.'

Nancy died in December 1986, just before Walter's eighty-eighth birthday. He arranged for her grave to be sited on the right-hand side at the top of the steps leading to the upper church yard, with the simple inscription, 'BA (Nancy) Pearse' and her dates. He was devoted to her. Once, delivering Mum a bar of chocolate, he brought out from under his pullover an old photograph of Nancy hidden there to protect it from the rain that morning. 'What do you think of that?' he asked Mum, proud of Nancy's youthful good looks.

'It is sad here with Mrs Pearse gone... I hope that this won't knock the stuffing out of Walter: sixty-seven years together is a great deal.'

In the summer Walter would sometimes cut Mum's grass when she was poorly or away visiting us, and she would do the same for him. He once told her, 'I'm thinking of having a row with you because you do too much for everyone.' Mum replied, 'If you did that I would move house.'

Walter took Mum in his car to visit Kathleen Short after she had moved to the nursing home at Hooe where she spent her last years. It was the last time the three of them were all together. Afterwards Mum walked into Hooe churchyard to visit the grave of her brother Arthur, and then Walter took Mum for a wonderful drive through the lanes, ending at Saltram House. 'Mr Pearse is ever so funny and made me laugh.'

Towards the end of his life, Walter told me insistently and repeatedly that he regarded Mum as some sort of saint. He spoke these words urgently to me. Mum's strenuous denials and confusion when he said this to her had not changed his mind. It was as if Walter was puzzled and searching after whatever it was that had made it possible for Mum to live in the way that he so respected. There was something completely sincere, heartfelt and touching in this tribute. It showed how much two people of completely different temperament and experience had come to value and esteem each other.

※

On her eighty-eighth birthday, in hospital, Mum was talking to me about Walter. She had six months still to live. She had received many birthday cards, and the nurses had sung 'Happy Birthday'.

'It's a good job the nurses are all so lovely,' she said. 'They'll live to make the world a better place. This is a lovely ward…'

Then, out of the blue, she added, 'Mr Pearse wasn't a lion. He was a lamb.'

31
A Pattern of Life

THERE WAS A PATTERN to our life in those years. I had the feeling that it would never end, neither for Mum nor for Judy and me.

Mum began to visit us in London after she had lost Rusty. Three times a year she came to stay with us. In time the visits fell back to two a year, then one, and finally, nearly twenty years later, they ceased altogether when 'Anno Domini' took control, as Mum put it.

Mum travelled light. Her belongings would be folded into a small mustard-coloured hold-all, bought in Ridgeway for £5. I would collect her at Paddington station on a Saturday afternoon in our Morris Minor 1000 and bring her home across London, trying to make the trip interesting: through Hyde Park, past the Serpentine, and along the edge of The Green Park, with a glimpse of Buckingham Palace, through St James's Park and past Big Ben and the Houses of Parliament, over the River Thames, and then quickly down the Old Kent Road and through New Cross to Lewisham. In those years the traffic on Saturday was often light and we used to have a clear run.

Judy would greet us. We would have tea beside the fire, the table laid with a patterned violet cloth, brought out especially for these Saturday afternoons. We would use the silver teapot and fine bone china, in Art Deco style, that Judy's mother had received as a wedding present in 1934.

Mum settled herself in the spare bedroom. On her bedside table she put a little leather wallet of photographs that she always carried in her handbag. In it there was a holiday snap of Dad on Challaborough beach, in an open-necked shirt and a long-sleeved pullover and grey flannel trousers. Mum called this picture of him 'Contemplation'. Opposite it was one of her with my brother and me, taken on holiday in the lane near the caravan.

Between the photos were a few Bible texts, which she had cut out over the years, chosen from those printed day by day at the head of the personal column in the *Daily Telegraph*:

> If God be for us, who can be against us?
> St Paul, Letter to the Romans, viii, 31
>
> Let not your hearts be troubled, neither let them be afraid
> St John's Gospel, xiv, 27
>
> Now the God of hope fill you with all joy and peace in believing, that you may abound in hope
> St Paul, Letter to the Romans, xv, 13

Occasionally Mum travelled up from home on a Friday. She enjoyed the excitement of arriving at Paddington station in the rush hour. Once she came a week early. She was proud that, in her late sixties, she had found her way across London, by tube and Southern Region train, and arrived safely at our house. Aghast, we recognised her tall, stocky form and the colours of her dark green and brown tweed winter coat and brown hat through the glass panels in the front door. 'Mother!' exclaimed Judy. She wanted to go home the next day but we persuaded her to stay.

On her return to Devon, Mum told her friends of her great adventure. Her pride was punctured by her old friend, Mary Bassett, the cub leader and doctor's receptionist, who retorted, 'Well, you've got a tongue in your 'ade, haven't you, Grace?'

When in April 1980 Jumble, a border terrier, entered our life, Mum's visits were transformed. Three times a day Mum took Jumble to Manor House Gardens, our local park. There she had long conversations with some of the regular dog-walkers.

She made friends with our neighbours in Thornwood Road, many of them of about her age. They shared their memories of the country before the Second World War. Mum enjoyed hearing from them of the romance and excitement of life in London in those distant days when she and Wally had visited Uncle Jack and Auntie Nellie.

Opposite us at number 29 lived Doris and Fred. Fred had worked as a commercial traveller. In retirement, he took up painting and produced an accurate and poignantly heartfelt watercolour of our house, the view that he and Doris had looked out on for all their married life, now with our Morris Minor standing in front of it.

For these neighbours and the dog-walking companions in the park, Mum's visits to us came to be like the periodic return of the swallow. She would call on them each time to say goodbye before going back to Plympton.

We used to take Mum to a play at the Greenwich Theatre, thriving at that time under the leadership of

Ewan Hooper and, after him, Alan Strachan. They achieved their great success by making demands of their audience. They devised a programme for both highbrow and middlebrow tastes, for example, Goldoni's *Artful Widow*, Wilde's *An Ideal Husband* and *A Woman of No Consequence*, and, by way of contrast, Sophocles' *Oedipus* plays. Most powerful of all, on a frosty winter's evening, was the performance of Euripides' *Trojan Women*, which we saw from the back row of the theatre, enthralled in a still, deep silence.

On Saturday we might take Mum for a drive in the country in Kent and East Sussex. We visited the garden at Sissinghurst Castle.

We might take her for a walk at Ide Hill, near Sevenoaks. Before the great storm of October 1987 the hill was crowned by a massive stand of beech trees. Below them to the south lay many acres of oak, ash and hornbeams where Jumble chased rabbits. In May there was a sea of bluebells. We had lunch by the fire in the village pub. Mum relished observing how the customers tackled their food ('that woman ate two pies, and, boy, did she enjoy them!'). Then we went home to the fireside at number 28, with a cup of tea, and perhaps a final walk with Jumble in Manor House Gardens.

On Sunday, Mum came with us to our local church for the service of Holy Communion. Sometimes we all went to Evensong.

In her hold-all Mum brought her well-worn blue Bible, and with it the prayers written on scraps of paper slipped in between its pages. She would make her prayers night and morning, and sometimes on the landing upstairs I would hear the quiet murmur of her saying them.

The days raced past. All the things that we could not normally do because we were out at work all day, we would find done for us when we got home in the evening. All my woollen socks would be beautifully darned, and Mum would do some weeding in the garden.

※

After Peggy's death in 1975 Judy missed out on the pleasure of visits that her mother would have made to stay with us. Perhaps her awareness of this made Mum even more grateful for the warm welcome Judy gave her.

In hospital, Judy was often in Mum's thoughts at the end of her life, happy thoughts and full of good memories.

'I've always loved Judy,' she told me. 'She's a godsend in an earthquake. Thank her for being a lovely daughter to me. She knows what to do in a predicament. Who can help loving her?'

※

The time would come for Mum to return home. At Paddington we bought her a copy of *Country Life* to read on the journey. If she left on a Saturday or Sunday, we settled her down in the first-class carriage where, for paying a one-pound supplement, she could travel on her second-class ticket.

Mum loved those rail journeys. Once, as she travelled through Berkshire, she saw a kingfisher – a flash of blue and burnt orange along the surface of the canal. She told us of her conversations at various times with a nun, an actress and, often, young people.

Back at number 10 she would thirstily enjoy her first full cup of tea for the day. She knelt in the kitchen by the Rayburn in order to light its oil burner. Occasionally Kathleen would come in from next door to see Mum.

Before she got into bed that night Mum wrote a short entry in her diary. 'John and Judy took me to Paddington... Very sad am I... Week in London restored me.' On another occasion she wrote, 'Lovely to be back in Dad's house.'

And to us she wrote:

> I was very sad to leave Jumble. He did not like it when I brought my bag downstairs... I thought your house and garden lovely, and I feel very much at home with you. Don't let that frighten you.

32
Time Passes

CHRISTMAS GAVE MUM JOY to the end of her life.

She loved the frantic atmosphere in the shops as everyone stocked up for the holidays. As long as her bachelor brothers Jack and George were alive, she made them a massive fruit cake, a plum pudding and a dozen mince pies. These she delivered to number 7 on Christmas Eve when they kept open house there for family and friends.

Over the decades her diaries record:

23rd November started puddings ...
1st December made mincemeat.

❄

In the weeks before the first of her three Christmases in hospital, Mum said to me, 'Everyone wants to be at home for Christmas ... It's lovely to be at home at Christmas.'

Perhaps she was hoping even then to get home to number 10 and spend Christmas there. It could not be.

❄

We often spent Easter with Mum, too.

On Easter Sunday we went to the eight o'clock service at St Mary's church with Mum and met all the regulars. After the service we walked up to the churchyard and visited Dad's grave, with its granite headstone near the boundary hedge. A robin sang. We sensed Dad with us. We tidied the grave a little, and put some flowers in a jam-jar by the headstone.

Mum told me that she wished her ashes to be laid there, with Dad, 'slipped into the grave so as not to disturb him'.

※

Mum loved St Mary's church, partly for all the memories of her wedding and many other family events, partly for its link with so many of her friends over a lifetime, and partly for the vicars and curates whom she had seen come and go.

In her handbag Mum kept a visiting-card left by Mr Mitchell, the vicar during the Second World War, when he had called on her at number 7, Stone Barton before she left for India with me in January 1946. 'Called to see Mother and Baby, but found you out,' Mr Mitchell had written in pencil, much faded over the years, but greatly treasured and often handled by Mum.

In the early 1980s Mum was amused by the novels of Barbara Pym, so many of which recorded incidents in the heroines' lives involving curates in London churches in the 1950s. Perhaps the role of curates in Plympton in the 1970s and 1980s was not all that different from what Miss Pym had observed in the suburbs of London thirty years earlier.

Mum came to know especially well one of them,

Peter Morgan, who was unusually 'High' for Plympton St Mary's and performed complex rituals at services. 'We have an unusual curate at St Mary's,' Mum wrote to me. 'He is very High Church... He has a lovely clear voice.'

> I will be having the curate to call soon. He swaggered along yesterday and called out, 'Coming to see you soon.' They say that he stays two hours. He travels around in a Mexican-type black hat and cape, and everyone in the shops seems to like him; quite a character. He sweeps off his hat to every lady.

Some of the congregation did not get used to Peter Morgan and his elaborate rituals. Mum was not 'High', but she was happy to take him as she found him. He did visit her, 'and we had a very interesting conversation. He is a very kind man indeed.'

Mum went on to enjoy many talks with him. Usually they met at the front gate when she was gardening and he was on his way to visit the shops or to take his letters to the post office. Mum once found him sitting on her garden wall, faint from the heat. She invited him into the house for a spoonful of brandy, which she kept for such occasions.

On another day, after visiting an old people's home, Mr Morgan told her about it and then shuddered and said, 'Disgusting.' Despite her own advanced age, Mum found his honesty refreshing and highly amusing. 'He's a funny chap and he makes me laugh.' Mum dreaded the possibility of becoming, as she put it, an 'inmate' of such an institution: 'I hope to avoid it a little longer. When I lose my determination, I shall be ready for 'Dickie's Meadow'.'

A little later Mr Morgan married a Plympton girl,

Ruth, a member of the church choir. Mum attended the wedding service.

Peter Morgan was as good a priest as he was a source of good humour. He showed that in 1982 when, unusually, Mum was alone at Easter.

The Argentinians had invaded the Falkland Islands, British territory, on Good Friday, the second of April. Mum's shock at the wanton, unprovoked attack became mixed with her religious feelings, prompted by Holy Week, and unsettled her. 'Cried much,' she wrote in her diary. She enjoyed the Easter services, but was very upset again on the following Tuesday. Peter Morgan visited her for a talk. In her diary Mum recorded around this time of Mr Morgan, 'He spoke to me very kindly,' and again that 'he called for a chat'. 'I have a great liking for him,' she told me.

A few days later Judy and I arrived for a weekend visit. Mum continued to be worried by the Falklands War. She recorded her fears and hopes: 'Bad news: two more losses,' on the seventh of May; 'Better news,' on the twelfth; 'Better news,' again on the twenty-ninth; and 'War over... white flag raised; great rejoicing; sad loss of life,' on the fourteenth and fifteenth of June.

Gradually, Mum regained her equilibrium during the summer. She was shaken when some MPs and papers and the BBC raked over the campaign. We talked about it. 'Our forces were marvellous and they stood up well for the poor islanders,' she wrote to me.

Roger Beck took over from Mr Morgan. Mum got to know him best of all the curates, especially in her last years.

※

Until her late seventies Mum came with us on good walks when we stayed with her. She and Judy would make a picnic, with pasties or sandwiches, fruit and an old blue thermos full of hot water for tea and coffee. We would gather together rugs and coats and hats, and, with Jumble, we would set off for the Devon countryside.

One of her favourites started at Plymbridge and followed the footpath up the course of the old branch-line railway from Marsh Mills junction beside the River Plym. Dad and Mum had taken us on an outing by train on that line to Yelverton and Princetown.

In summer we went to walk by the sea in the South Hams. We parked near the 'Journey's End' pub at Ringmore and walked down the steep footpath to Ayrmer cove, the 'Magic Beach' of our childhood holidays in the caravan at Challaborough. We had a swim, followed by chocolate cake and a cup of tea on a beach as deserted and beguiling as any visited by Odysseus on his wanderings, about which I had read, there by the sea, when I devoured Homer's works as a schoolboy.

After the picnic we walked back to the village and ate an ice-cream from the village shop, sitting in the graveyard of All Hallows church. With Dad's binoculars we looked out to sea and searched for the Eddystone lighthouse on the horizon. Then we drove back to number 10 for a cup of tea in the back garden. On our way home we would sing one or two of Mum's pantomime songs.

After one of our visits, Mum wrote to Judy and me:

You make my life complete,
Gee, but you're awful sweet...

Of course, the trouble with such happy visits is that they come to an end. Time was passing. Time also ends.

※

Life grew harder for Mum.

Her old friends noticed the change. 'Fancy you ending up like this, Grace,' said one of those who had worked with her at Yeo's when they met at the shops in Ridgeway. 'You'm still alive, then, Grace,' said another, in the broad Devon idiom. A third asked her, 'Are you or Wally the elder, Grace?'

'Rather flattering,' she wrote to me.

Mum loved to joke with us about these comments, but things really were changing.

The population of Plympton had grown to twenty-four thousand by 1985, and was still growing. When the city of Plymouth achieved the ambition that it had long nursed of extending eastwards, it smothered Plympton. The life and identity of an ancient Devonshire village were being rubbed out. Some of the arrivals tried to hold on to the way of life that had attracted them in the first place but Plympton and, with it, Moorland Road became less peaceful.

※

Uncle George's health had been growing worse for years. After his brother Jack died in March 1976, Mum often visited George to clean the house and spend some time with him. 'I love it,' she told me. She made him a steak-and-kidney pie. George said, 'It was the first I have eaten since Mother died in 1943.'

She came to understand the efforts that Jack had made to keep house for himself and George.

> Since I began working at number 7 I have a close insight into Uncle Jack's character. He was pretty good in achieving what he did, and he was struggling against great odds. Jack had been poorly for some time before he died.

In December 1985 George died of a stroke. He was eighty-three years old. Mum and Fred organised the funeral. They cleared out number 7, on which no real work had been done in the forty years since Mum had left it in January 1946 to join Dad in India, taking me with her.

George's death and the spartan conditions in which he had lived preyed on Mum's mind for many months.

> He could have had quite a different life if he had gone into the Army, but no one encouraged him. If you don't have someone to encourage you, you don't bother. He used to keep all sad things under concrete blocks. But other people can't be responsible for you.
>
> Everyone always wanted to help George. In hospital, after his stroke, all the nurses wanted to care for him. 'I'll bath George,' they used to say.

It was only at midsummer that Mum recovered her spirits. 'I played the piano yesterday,' she told me, 'the first time since George died.'

※

Mum spoke to Wally or Audrey every day on the telephone. They occasionally took her out for a drive, until they gave up their car. The frequent contact could be a mixed blessing. 'George was much more jolly than they are,' she said. When they took her on a trip in the sun to the moors near Cornwood, 'Their conversation was deeply depressing, as usual... I took all night and half of yesterday to get over it.'

Mum made light of what was happening. She said she was afraid of becoming what her old friend Lily Coombes, in their youth, had called one of the older staff at Yeo's – 'a bitter weed'.

Mum went on some wonderful drives with her nephew Jack and his wife Phyllis. One drive on Dartmoor brought back memories of her honeymoon.

> At Holne Chase I had a good look at Church Inn as Dad and I had bread and cheese and a Coxes apple there. He had a glass of beer and I had a glass of lemonade on our honeymoon. Very nostalgic! It was rationing days, of course, then.

Uncle Fred became ill in the late summer of 1987. In December he had to move into a residential home. It was difficult for him. Fred dearly loved his own home. During the Second World War he had sent a verse to Hilda from Germany, setting it to a tune of his own:

> Everybody loves their little home,
> And I love mine,
> It's so divine.
> I often wonder why I went to roam
> So far across the mighty foam.
> It matters not how long I've been away-
> Come home some day,
> I hope and pray-
> No one seems to grumble if it's rich or humble –
> Everybody loves their little home.

Mum became distressed that she could not do more for Fred.

Mr and Mrs Kelly, the old friends who kept the little grocery shop in Ridgeway, retired at the end of 1988. The shop's new owners did not sell groceries.

In January 1990 Walter Pearse, who had gone to stay with his daughter and her family for Christmas, did not return. He nursed the hope that he might be able to return in the summer, but it was not to be.

In July 1990 Fred died. He had been unhappy in the home. Once during those two and a half years, Mum wrote, 'Fred actually smiled today.' After his death Mum often recorded in her diary: 'I miss Fred.'

※

Mum's visits to stay with us in London went down from three to two a year, and then to one. She stayed with us for the last time, both in London and at our cottage in East Sussex, at the end of May 1991. It was bluebell time. We walked slowly in the woods and enjoyed their colour and heady smell on the slope bordering the River Limden. On Bank Holiday Monday Mum managed to come to a barbeque party given by our neighbour.

At the cottage Mum admired my work on the vegetable patch. 'I always said you would be happier hoeing turnips than doing anything else,' she reminded me. 'It's a fine job, although people don't think so these days.' And she quoted:

> The cure for this ill is not to sit still,
> Or doze with a book by the fire,
> But to take a large hoe and a large fork,
> And dig till you gently perspire.

The following Wednesday Judy took her to Paddington for the last time to return to Plymouth. On the drive to the station she caught a final glimpse of the Serpentine where she had steered the boat erratically as Wally had rowed, sixty-five years earlier.

Kathleen Short died in October 1991. In her will she bequeathed Mum her barometer; and she left me Gordon's wing armchair.

33
'Gone are the days...'

IN HER TWENTY-THREE YEARS at number 10 after Dad's death Mum fed on the memories of what had made us all happy there over the years. She preserved the stories handed down within her family; what had been the first words of each of her brothers and sisters; family jokes; and comic and embarrassing incidents, often brought out with wicked glee and to telling effect, when nephews and nieces visited her with their spouses to whom the stories were new. She remembered the films that she had seen with her mother; the books she had read; and the words and tunes of songs that she had sung as a little girl at the pantomime each Christmas, as a sheet with the words painted on it was lowered above the stage.

'I try to accept old age gracefully and avoid being a bitter weed,' she wrote to me.

> I've had some great times...
> As Dad used to say
>   'Life is very sweet, brother;
>   there is night and day, brother, both sweet things;
>   sun, moon and stars, brother, all sweet things;

> there is likewise a wind on the heath,
> life is very sweet, brother'[6]
>
> I look back on my visits to you in London when you used to take me to Ide Hill with Jumble, and the majestic ring of beech trees, and the sausage and chips and tomatoes at the Inn, and the viburnum growing in the hedge...
>
> I remember the journeys back to dear old number 10 on the train, seeing the kingfisher on the canal in Wiltshire and all the primroses in the fields and hedges and railway embankments as we reached Devon...
>
> I am sad at not being with you on your birthday. It's difficult now that my legs are such a nuisance. I guess that my travelling days are coming to a close...
>
> All good things come to an end...

A few weeks later, just before her eighty-second birthday, Mum wrote to us again.

> This is a very sad letter for me, as I love to come to visit you in London and the cottage but it is no good. I cannot face the three- or four-hour journey... This letter is short, but I am sad.

On the same day in her diary she made a short note: 'John rang. He understands.'

'London can be very beautiful,' she wrote to us later.

> I remember Judy taking me to the Serpentine in autumn on the way to Paddington when huge leaves covered the ground. Jumble was rushing around chasing the leaves.

The telephone became even more important to us.

---

6 Based on words of George Borrow in *Lavengro*, Chapter 25, which were reproduced on a small water-colour of heather in flower on Dartmoor which hung beside the fireplace in the dining room at number 10 for many years.

Judy would hear gales of laughter at my end of the line as she prepared our supper. There would be funny stories about odd incidents, or the quirky characters that Mum had met or observed going about their business in Ridgeway, or some comments made to her. But it was Mum's general attitude and humour rather than the jokes that caused the laughter. With the same temperament we knew at once what would help or encourage the other, especially laughter.

※

When she reached eighty-three years, Mum could get to St Mary's only when we were staying with her. She was afraid to accept the lifts that the other 'eight o'clockers' offered her, in case she caught her bad leg on the door of a strange car.

At first she also turned down the clergy's offer to celebrate the Holy Communion for her at home. It would have meant that she had accepted that her old way of life was over and done with, and that she would never get to church again. But, at last, she agreed when Roger Beck suggested that he should come on a Wednesday afternoon once a month and celebrate the service with her. Mum came to love those occasions. Roger would spread a little white cloth on her side-table near the fireplace in the sitting-room, and would place on it a lighted candle, her prayer-book, together with a small Communion chalice for the wine and a patten for wafers. Afterwards Mum and Roger would sit by the fire for a while and talk.

※

In November 1993 Wally died. A month later, Walter Pearse followed him. After he had moved away to live with his daughter, he and Mum had often talked on the telephone. In this way Mum had felt he was still next door.

Walter bequeathed to Mum the Victorian wrought-iron garden seat on which they had often sat together and talked.

The following February Mum came on a short walk with me in the pathfields leading to St Maurice. We took a thermos with us. We found the first celandines shining at the foot of the lime trees planted there to celebrate Queen Victoria's diamond jubilee. We watched a wren and a robin building their nests in the hedge by the slate wall. We knew that this would be Mum's last real walk, in a spot that she had always loved. A man and his wife, passing through the pathfields to the shops in Ridgeway, took a photograph of us sitting on the bench as we drank a cup of coffee. Mum became more or less housebound but was still able to take care of herself there with help from Betty and her husband Glen who had helped Walter and Nancy.

When we visited Mum, we found ourselves doing more and more to help her to keep going between visits. Mum hated our 'working for her' (as she put it) but the thought of leaving number 10, where she had lived for so long with Dad, was anathema to her. Every night she used to say 'goodnight' to him, stepping into the enormous cupboard under the stairs, and gently touching his last trilby hat, still hanging on one of the pegs there. These memories and associations kept her going.

'Getting up is a slow business, but I get there in the end. Today I rose at 6.30 and have just finished breakfast at 10.30.'

In her own mind, Mum was ready for death. She loved life. She felt that she was lucky in her family and friends, but I now know better than I then did how much pain and loneliness she suffered in her last ten years.

Mum did not fear death. She feared judgement, but she knew that beyond judgement lies God's mercy, each somehow giving meaning to the other. She had a strong sense that life continued through death.

In her last couple of years at number 10, Mum had two unusual experiences, which puzzled her. She did not make much of them. To me, it seemed that she was living somehow in the borderland between this world and the next. We were to find ourselves spending a lot of time together in those regions.

On the first of these two occasions, Mum was in bed. It was as if her mother were in the bedroom with her, standing over her. Mum reached up to kiss her and said, 'Don't worry.' Puzzled and a little alarmed at what was happening, Mum switched on the light. She did not know whether it was a dream or some other sort of experience that she had never had before. She told me that it had felt quite different from the dream that she had had the previous night, about her mother and father and her seven brothers and sisters, all together at number 7, Stone Barton.

On the second occasion, Mum was sitting in her armchair beside the fire in the sitting-room. She had a dream in which she and my brother and I were in the kitchen by the Rayburn.

Suddenly, Dad came down the stairs, fit and well, dancing and singing, and we all joined in the dance.

In the days at 'Babworth', our bungalow at St Ives, wearing his old corduroy trousers and pullover and trilby hat, Dad used to lead us in a dance through the bungalow and around the garden, past the tulips and wallflowers and, later, in the summer, the lupins which did so well there. Dad would sing and we would join in.

Mum awoke, and she had a continuing strong sensation that Dad was in the chair at the other side of the fireplace, where he always used to sit, next to the piano.

※

In April 1994 Mum passed out when she was sitting at the kitchen table after breakfast. Her old friends Nan Matthews and Betty Peters realised that something was amiss and saved her life. In hospital it was discovered that she needed an operation, which took place in September.

Judy took a week's leave from school in October and looked after her when she came home after her stay in hospital. After their week together, Mum wrote:

Judy spoiled me...
I miss Judy...
I'm here at number 10. Thanks be to God.

She wrote to us, 'Simple pleasures are the best of all. I will endeavour to accept things gracefully, and am sorry to worry you... I will not deny that I like being here in this house. The sun is shining, the sky is blue, the garden and house are tidy, I have had a good breakfast by the Rayburn and there is a lovely late rose on the window sill.'

Mum made a good recovery and did give in about some things. We went there for Christmas, but this time we did most of the work. We made the Christmas puddings according to her recipe, written down for us in 1991 when we first did it together:

> 3 lbs each of washed raisins, sultanas and currants;
> half lb skinned almonds to chop;
> quarter lb of suet;
> 1 lb plain white flour;
> 2 big Bramley apples;
> mixed spices (ground ginger, mixed candied peel, ground nutmeg, cinnamon)
> bottle of stout;
> six eggs;
> one orange;
> one lemon;
> soft brown sugar.

The battered preserving-pan came out, the old recipe was followed, and we all stirred the mixture, and then cooked it on the Rayburn for seven or eight hours. After we left she wrote, 'The puddings look very good in the larder. I have to put clean greaseproof paper and foil on each one – which reminds me, did I pay for the greaseproof and foil?'

In the days before Christmas we took over the shopping. We gave ourselves over to making life the same as it had been since Dad died. In Job's words, 'If only I could go back to the old days.' Mum used to sing, to the same effect, the spiritual from the cotton fields of the Deep South: 'Gone are the days when my heart was young and gay...'

In her diary she wrote some fateful words of Edward FitzGerald, perhaps by her mistakes in some of the words even adding power to these lines in the *Rubaiyat of Omar Khayyam*:

> The moving finger writes
> And having writ moves on;
> And neither piety nor wit
> Can cancel out a line.

In February 1995 Florrie, Dad's last remaining sister, died.

At Easter we stayed with Mum. We managed to take her to eight o'clock Holy Communion. The strain was telling on her. On the following day she wrote, 'John and Judy gone. Sad.'

The pace quickened. I visited her every four or five weeks. Judy and I both stayed with her at Whitsun. Mum would write something in her diary after these visits:

> Lovely time. John gone. Sad ...
> John here. Good. Lovely three days ...
> I cooked dinner. We sat in garden. Very hot ...
> Lovely time with John and Judy.

At the end of July and in early August, Judy and I took a holiday in the North. The heat was stifling over all the country. One evening when we telephoned Mum, she was very confused, fluently producing non-existent but uncannily plausible words and phrases. On a Sunday evening, in the middle of August, we arrived at number 10 to spend a week with her. In her diary Mum recorded what we did that week, as her spirits rose day by day.

Mum looked well when we left.

As the years had passed, Mum felt the benefit of our visits for a shorter and shorter period after we left. The last entries that she made in her diary were on Sunday the tenth of September.

On the morning of Monday the eleventh Mum was sitting at the breakfast table in the kitchen, writing her weekly letters.

'The greatest sadness is when you can't write letters any more,' she said to me a year later, in hospital. 'I always tried to write something, even when nothing interesting happened in the week. As Dad said, "Habit is ten times nature."'

Midway through a sentence in her letter to Judy and me Mum slumped forward onto the table.

As had happened eighteen months earlier, Mum's friend Nan had decided to call on her on Monday morning that week because she was not able to make her regular visit on the Tuesday.

But this Monday Nan looked through the glass in the inner front door down the passage to the kitchen and again she realised that something had gone wrong. She contacted Roger Triscott, the local builder who had taken such good care of number 10 for so many years. He got into the house through the sitting-room window, and for the second time Mum's life was saved by her good friends. They called an ambulance to take her, unconscious, to hospital. Three weeks later she had a stroke. She never left hospital.

Through these two good friends Providence was watching over Mum and our whole family.

34
'What can't be cured…'

MUM WAS TAKEN ILL three weeks before I left one job and became self-employed. That change was to prove my liberation. Mum helped me to cross my own Styx from one way of life to another.

Suddenly I was more or less the master of my diary and time. I could spend a lot of time on visits to Mum. I went there on seventy-three trips between October 1995 and May 1998. Twenty-two of the visits were day trips, and fifty-one lasted for three or more days. Judy came when she could.

※

Today I am on my own.

'Good afternoon, Mother.'

'Good afternoon, John. I've been expecting you. I prayed that you'd come and now you are here. It often happens. When you came in I got the same old thrill.'

I pull up a chair and arrange my belongings. I go along to the cupboard in the entrance hall and take out a vase, fill it with water at the hand-basin near Mum's bed, and do my best with the flowers.

When I am staying at number 10 I can bring flowers from Mum and Dad's garden, their flowers: violets, camellias, celandines, viburnum, New Dawn roses, bluebells, apple blossom, lilac, and kaffir lilies. But any flowers are welcome to Mum in hospital, especially those that are sweet-smelling; and above all, freesias.

Carefully, I bring them over for Mum to smell.

'Lovely.'

Mum asks after Judy, who is working at school today. She always asks after Judy straightaway.

'I remember collecting chestnuts with her in Greenwich Park... And blackberries. I wouldn't want to be a blackberry if Judy were around... I've always loved Judy. Judy holds our family together...'

Mum goes over so many incidents and conversations that she has had with Judy over the years.

She remembers her own mother.

'Poor old Mother, I was such a baby. She loved Christmas. On Christmas Eve, as she was making mince-pies, and lots of visitors were coming and going, she used to drink a glass of stout, and she would put a red-hot poker in it to warm it up if it was a freezing day.

'She always looked so smart on Christmas Day in the new clothes we had given her. I used to enjoy going to Pophams, with its thick carpet and its glass counters with their wooden drawers, and buying her a lovely blouse.

'We had so many happy times... I do hope that Mother enjoyed her life. I hope that so much.

'At the end of her life, in the War, she was lying ill in bed, in the Blitz, and then she opened her eyes and said, "Do stop looking at me so much, Grace!"

'She told me not to cry for her when she'd gone. "Regain your equilibrium," was how she put it.

'And she just slipped away. I went downstairs from the bedroom, leaving her asleep, and then, when I went up again, she'd gone.

'Mother left me £8 and her rosewood writing table…

'While I was in India with Dad and you, Jack and George stained the table with their shaving tackle, but it came up all right when I polished it.

'She kept all her treasures and presents in a pink satin box. It had four legs, and had been a chocolate-box. She had a few little pieces of jewellery. Jack and George threw away the pink satin box, although I'd put all of Dad's letters in it for safe-keeping, tied in bundles with ribbon… They were very rough-and-ready, down-to-earth men…

'I'd give anything to see Mother, just for five minutes…'

And gently, half under her breath, Mum sings the song, *Love is the Sweetest Thing…*

She drifts into silence for a while.

※

Mum suddenly looks me straight in the eye.

'I'm not ruining your life, am I?'

'You're a lovely part of our life.'

Mum smiles broadly.

'Don't smarm me, will you? Life is difficult, especially when you've got an old woman of eighty-seven for your mother.'

We laugh a lot.

'You mustn't gild me over. I'm fed up with me, a bad tempered old sinner…'

※

The nurses come to make Mum more comfortable, and to turn her onto her right side. We know them so well now.

It is as if we have always known them. It is as if this life that we share with them will never end; but it will.

I walk along the ward and have a word with one or two of the patients and some of the nurses. In the day-room, where the more active patients can sit and read or watch television, I gaze out of the window and look at the estuary of the River Plym.

At low tide there is a wide expanse of sand, smooth and sparkling, laid down over the years by the waste of quartz and feldspar carried there by a moorland brook from the china clay works at Lee Moor. It stretches from the Plymouth side of the river to the woods that lead up from the rocky shoreline to Saltram House. This afternoon there is a high tide and the blue, slightly choppy waters glisten in the early afternoon sun. Once or twice, in her first year here, I was able to take Mum outside in a wheel chair, so that she could feel the breeze on her cheeks and see the wonderful view.

No one is in the day-room today. There are pictures on the walls and a bookcase, with a vase of paper flowers standing on it. It has the atmosphere of a sitting-room, frozen at some date in the 1970s, when the patients here and most of the visitors would have been in their late middle-age, still able to run their own home and enjoying life, with grown-up children and, perhaps, young grandchildren. Everything about the room seems to fit in here, and it is a comfort.

35

'The best thing that ever happened to me…'

THE CURTAINS AROUND Mum's bed rustle and are drawn back.

'I loved it when Dad laughed. I loved to hear his Cornish jokes and to hear him laugh… He loved the joke about the man selling newspapers who used to call out "*News of the World* – and all the other places"… I'd love to see him and hear him have a good laugh now.

'He used to say, "O what a troubled web we weave, When first we practise to deceive."

'Everything that Dad planned worked out well. If only I had let Dad guide everything, it would all have been better. I went in where angels feared to tread. How much he loved you boys. He was so proud of you both…

'Dad was generous and gentle, always on the side of the loser. He was the best thing that ever happened to me…

'On one of our first walks when we were courting, we had lunch at the Skylark Inn at Clearbrook. Dad had a bread roll and cheese. I can see him eating it now… I was overjoyed that, later on, he let me buy him a pint of beer. I had lemonade... Dad proposed to me at Lee Moor Gate, on the edge of Dartmoor...

'In India, he loved to have "rumble tumble" for breakfast, sitting with me on the verandah. That's what he called scrambled egg. He used to break the brittle toast into pieces by putting the flat of his hand on it, on the plate... Dad looked so lovely there in his officer's uniform...

'Our garden was full of flowers. The mali used to water them every day... Beautiful Indian schoolgirls used to walk past the bungalow in their school uniforms and we would hear them singing...

'Wasn't it lovely when we lived at Venton Cottage? I used to put you both in the pram, and push you up the lane by the wood. We'd all meet Dad off the bus at Sparkwell coming back from Plymouth with the weekly shopping, and then we'd walk together down that wonderful lane to the cottage and the fire, and kippers for tea...

'We had a lovely garden at the bungalow at St Ives. Dad loved working in it and cleaning out the chicken-run. There was a big border of lupins and dahlias.

'On Guy Fawkes Night Dad ran around the garden with sparklers to entertain you...

'He went up to Plympton to look for a house and he found number 10 Moorland Road. It was convenient in every way for us, and for you both to go to Plymouth College...

'Dad was always keen for you boys to go there. He was very clever, and got his Higher National Certificates in the Army. You made us both burst with pride with all you did at Oxford...

'Do you remember the little barrel of cider that Dad

used to have standing by the door in the kitchen each Christmas... and the bottle of Dry Fly sherry that you used to buy him for his birthday? And how he used to buy you both raspberry and banana milkshakes at Mr Crooks' shop when we were at the caravan at Challaborough?

'Don't forget all the lovely outings with Dad, the walks, and train rides, and Paignton Zoo, and the theatre, and picking whortleberries at Princetown on Dartmoor... Take good care of Dad's M.B.E.

'Later on [when Mum says this, she means the time when Dad was suffering from Huntington's chorea], he and I loved picking up chestnuts at Windwhistle Wood with Rusty. Dad loved doing that.

'I thanked Dad for a lot of things a couple of days ago when I was going through them all, for more than ever before... I'm so glad that I have him for my husband...

'He was lovely, wasn't he?

'I'm looking forward to seeing Dad again. He was a lovely husband and father... He was the best thing that ever happened to me. I was almost too happy with him, but I didn't have long enough with Dad, only twenty-eight years...' And Mum's face takes on a special tender look. And for a while all is quiet around us in the ward, with the nurses walking to and fro, and their footsteps muffled by the springy grey linoleum, and the sun shining across the floor and the beds, and no one speaks.

The afternoon is beginning to slip away.

36
'A Ring of Faithfulness'

MUM STILL GETS lots of visitors.

There is no one of her generation still alive in the family, but my brother and his wife, Mum's nephews and nieces, and Dad's, come to see her when they can. Friends from Plympton visit.

But two people, both in their mid-sixties, have emerged as Mum's most frequent visitors.

From Mum's side of the family there is her niece Mavis, Edie's daughter. She was widowed many years ago and is now sixty-five years old, not in wonderful health but still walking on Dartmoor, swimming in the sea off Plymouth Hoe, and reading and writing poetry. She is always full of fun and often has the patients and staff in uproar with her jokes.

And from Dad's side of the family there is his nephew, Jack, Florrie's second son. He was born in the same cottage as Dad in Jack Lane in Newlyn and was named after him. As a little boy, Jack wrote regularly to Dad in India. Jack is very fond of music, singing in his choir, poetry and the German language. In his fine copper-plate hand he used to write out poems from his favourite authors for Mum.

Both Jack and Mavis love the corny jokes that are so dear to Mum and so powerful in raising her spirits. One or other of them is often with Mum when I visit her. They work out between them when they will visit, a roster to ensure that Mum has a visitor as often as possible. I have seen the way that they take care of her. They treat her like a mother.

On one occasion, when the nurses were delivering Mum her supper and she looked disgusted with it, Mavis said, 'It's lovely,' and pretended to begin to eat it.

'That's Mavis's style of getting me to eat,' Mum told me. 'Give me a reason why I should say it's lovely because Mavis says it is,' but she began to drink the soup and to reminisce.

Often Mum and Mavis sing together and they enjoy themselves a lot. 'Silly songs,' Mum says, 'A load of rubbish, like "Bye, Bye Blackbird".' They sing deliberately flat, and laugh.

'We're very much alike, Mavis and I,' Mum says. 'Both daft. When I saw Mavis and Debbie, the nurse, whispering together, I called them "the wicked women's club", and, boy, did they laugh! They had been worrying about me, but, when I made that joke, they knew that I was all right.'

'Jack told me that he'll never leave me, he'll keep coming right till the end,' Mum told me one day. 'In the old days he used to take me from number 10 to Plymbridge to see the kingfisher, and he told me the other day that, from now on, he'll remember me every time that he crosses the bridge. He'll touch the bridge and pray for me. He's such a dear. He said, "You're never going to get rid of me. I'll keep visiting you wherever you are." He could see that I needed comfort.'

Then, as the end came near, Mum said, 'Jack came, and immediately everything was all right...'

At the end, when Mum could no longer speak, she gave Mavis a deliberate, slow wink, as if bidding her farewell and thanking her for all the laughter they had shared.

'I don't know what I'd do without Jack and Mavis. They are a ring of faithfulness...

'The world would be a sad place without the Mavises and Jacks... And it's not over when I'm gone. The family is still there, and everyone has still got to be connected with each other...

'I love Mavis and Jack, and they know it... I told them.'

※

Roger Beck, the curate from St Mary's, glides quietly around the corner into Mum's bay. Her face lights up and she welcomes him, 'I didn't know that it was Wednesday.'

During Mum's three years in hospital, Roger used to come to Ward 12 to celebrate Holy Communion with her. He would bring a special service sheet, with the main parts of the service printed boldly in big type on one page of paper. Mum could hold it in her right hand.

Mum asks him to use one of her favourite prayers at our service today:

O God, who hast prepared for them that love Thee
Such good things as pass man's understanding,

> Send into our hearts such love toward Thee
> That we, loving Thee above all things,
> May obtain Thy promises which exceed all we can
> desire, Through Jesus Christ, Our Lord. Amen.

She attends intently as Roger leads the service and joins in the prayers and says 'Amen' strongly and firmly. Afterwards, while Mum has a talk with Roger, I go for a walk down the ward.

When Roger has left, Mum says to me, 'Lovely things happen through being a Christian. Being in church makes you happy. It would be nice to have Jack here for the service. He prays with me, too.'

When the time came, it was Roger who gave Mum the last Christian rites, Holy Communion and anointing with holy oil. He saw her safely on her final journey to the life of the world to come.

※

What Mum endured in those thirty months sorely tested her. Some things, like being given a bath, were almost more than she could bear. Her bones ached, and her fragile skin grazed against the bath, pinching her. It made her cry. Sometimes her faith supported her, sometimes she felt troubled.

'I didn't think that life would end like this, did you?' she said. 'I thought it would phase out easily.'

Once she said to me, 'Where is Jesus? How can He help me? Where is He?'

Another time, she told me, 'I haven't felt the Lord for a while.'

And, again, 'Why should God treat me thus? I'm in a black tunnel, and I've got to come out of it. It's driving me mad. I don't feel I've done anyone any wrong. Why should I have to go through this?'

There is no answer.

The occasional despair passed, and Mum again felt God's presence in a comforting way. She prayed for 'peace at the last'.

She told me, 'I've been through some awful things, but it hasn't all been awful. It all depends on Jesus. He's the only way to get through everything.'

Mum never gave up praying for us all. 'I want you both to be really healthy and well. I pray for that all the time. It's like an ache, an ache in my throat.'

Remembering the kingfisher at Plymbridge, she said, 'Never mind. We've got to leave this world sometime. Thanks be to God for the glory of it.'

She saw all good things as signs of God's presence. 'I've been thinking of apple blossom,' she told me once, just as I arrived; and, again, 'I've been thinking about the ponies on Dartmoor.'

'People come around the door and restore my faith,' she told me. 'If I ever did anything right in my life, it was by accident. "Remember not our sins, O Lord." The terrible thing about life is what you ought to have done and did not do... Jesus is our Rock and Salvation... There is only God. You've just got to put your trust in Him. I try to... Prayers help us to get through life.'

One day in the early months I took Mum to the day-room in a wheel-chair. I gave her lunch as we looked across the estuary. At the end of our talk Mum closed her eyes for a while. Opening them, she said, 'Help me, Dear Lord, to go on my way rejoicing.' Again, she told me, 'I prayed, "O, Lord, forgive me for not continuing to be positive."' We often prayed the Lord's Prayer together at the end of visits.

On another occasion Mum told me, 'I dreamt that I was at my own funeral. I said to everyone, "Don't be sad. I'm on my way to my Lord Jesus."' Quoting hymns, she said, 'Jesu, lover of my soul...

'I heard the voice of Jesus say, "Come unto me and rest"...

'Jesus, the very thought of Thee with sweetness fills the breast...

'Don't cry for me. I'm ready to go on my way to my Lord Jesus. Nothing is impossible where Jesus is concerned... It'll be all right as long as Jesus gets us right in the end... He's got a big job to do.'

Jesus had been absolutely the centre of Dad's faith. During his years in India, Dad had underlined in pencil the name of Jesus in the first line of many of the hymns in his hymnbook, making a note of when each was sung at St Peter's church, Saugor. The talk about Jesus takes Mum's mind back to Dad.

'I wonder what Dad's doing now...'

※

Time is racing on.

'I hate it when you start collecting your belongings together to go,' Mum says.

'I'm not quite ready to die yet. I'll have to part with you all, but one day we'll all be together again.

'I hope that you'll bring Judy with you next time, and that you'll be able to go to the Magic Beach, and have a dip... I think about those days on holiday at the caravan all the time.'

Mum nods towards the photograph of Dad, standing on the beach, empty after everyone else has gone home, looking out to sea.

'I call that picture "Contemplation",' she says.

> Romans viii, 31.
> "If God be for us, who can be against us?"

> St. John 14, 27.
> "Let not your hearts be troubled, neither let them be afraid."

And then she looks at a postcard, propped on her bedside table, from Mr and Mrs Vicary, and their children, Robert and Carol. We used to meet them every summer for ten years at the caravan.

'I wish they were nearer,' she says. 'Very faithful people. I love their faithfulness, like comrades in a war.

> Comrades when danger was near
> Faithful whatever betide;
> Whenever dangers appear
> My comrade is there, by my side…

'Faithful friends, and a happy family... Dear God, forgive me, and help me to be worthy of it ...'

※

And this is what Mum and Dad taught me.

St Paul, reflecting on what he learnt through God's revelation to him in Jesus Christ, wrote that of the three great virtues – faith, hope and love – the third is the greatest; but without courage and loyalty they are nothing.

That is what they taught me.

※

My time is spent. I pack my belongings in my canvas London Library bag.

'You're a very tidy person,' Mum says. 'Thank you for all the loving care you've shown me...

'This is a lovely ward. They are all such dears...'

And, with a final wave, I slip away and rush down the stairs to the taxi booked to take me to the station, and so back to London. On the train I sleep deeply.

And none of us, and none of the doctors or nurses, can tell how long this will continue.

The months slip by, thirty-two months in all.

37
A Last Gift

ON MY VISITS I never know what to expect. As I walk along the corridor towards Mum's room I try to be silent and invisible. Today I manage it. All the nurses are far away at the other end of the ward. As I creep up to the door of Mum's room, I hear music. It comes from an old black and white television set. The nurses switch it on when Mum is in the mood, and today it is playing quietly.

Mum loves old films. She is chuckling to herself contentedly and peacefully. I stand outside the door for a while and listen. Mum suddenly gives her infectious laugh, a completely happy and healthy sound, and from the television there is the pained cry, 'Mr Grimsdale...'

It is Norman Wisdom's voice. He is starring in one of his films, made in the 1950s or early 1960s, which have given us so much joy at home over the years.

Mum and I watch the last few minutes of the film together before we begin to talk; then she has a sleep.

Three Christmases have passed. The end of Mum's life is drawing near.

After ten minutes or so, Mum opens her eyes. Even this takes an effort now. Slowly she manages to focus on my face, and then on the flowers, and then again on me.

'Good afternoon, Mother,' I say. This ritual has sustained us for thirty months. For a moment, there is a flicker of a smile, but today no words.

Mum's head rests on the white pillows, and her eyes half close. I sit there beside her, and the quiet, concentrated activity continues in the ward.

Then Mum's eyes open wide and she looks directly at me. Without being able to make a sound, she suddenly mouths some unexpected words to me:

'Two more for the Russians.'

And those are Mum's last words to me. I cannot restrain my laughter and it echoes down the ward. It is a joke that goes back forty-five years to early 1953, to the terrible days when Stalin still ruled in Russia and controlled Eastern Europe; when millions of Russians and others worked as slaves in Communist concentration camps. In a way, they were the lucky ones. Forty million people or more had already died because of him. He threatened us with a similar fate.

On an afternoon in February that year, a few months before the Queen's Coronation, when I was seven and my brother five, we stood after school at Mum's side in Mrs Willcocks's sweet-shop in Ridgeway. As her dour, withdrawn son served us with lemon sherbets, he looked down at the two of us and uttered the sinister comment, 'Two more for the Russians'. It was a month before Stalin's death.

And those words, so macabre in themselves and in their original intent, we turned into a joke that never failed us over the years. It is Mum's last gift to me in this life.

Sister Val and one or two of the other nurses and Marie, the tea lady with her trolley, bustle up to our corner. They are puzzled and look at me uncertainly. Then they see Mum's eyes shining with joy and triumph as she watches me laugh. It is impossible to explain the meaning of this laughter to Sister Val and the others. For a moment they smile at us, and then drift back to their work.

Mum's head settles back on the pillows and her eyes close. She sleeps for the rest of my visit.

On the way home I write:

> Ward 12,
> Mount Gould Hospital
>
> I hang between life and death,
> And life calls
> And death calls,
>
> And which I should choose
> I know not,
> I will not.
>
> I rest in the hands of God,
> And man must
> Wait and pray.

38
'Such sweet sorrow'

FOR TWO AND A HALF YEARS I found a unique escape, a release from all the tension that we went through, in my Russian language lessons, in what one of my teachers called 'the Russian music of words'. On Monday or Wednesday I used to go up to London to attend my classes with a succession of brilliant teachers. They always refreshed me.

On the first Wednesday in May 1998, after half a day's work, I felt jaded and off colour. I went home and wandered around the house listlessly. Something stopped me from going up to London for my conversation class. Normally, I would have felt sure that seeing Sasha our teacher and all the members of the class would lift my spirits, but that afternoon I decided against going.

Soon after five o'clock, Sister Val telephoned to say that Mum might not last long. Judy took me in the car the few hundred yards to our local station, and I just managed to catch the last express train from Paddington to Plymouth, the 7.35. I treated myself to dinner in the restaurant car. On the margin of a page of the newspaper I was reading, I wrote Dad's words to Mum in January 1945, when he left her in London after their honeymoon to return to India, 'Parting is such sweet sorrow.' I tore off the scrap of paper and put it in my jacket pocket. I found it months later.

At Newton Abbot the train was delayed for a while when a drunk accosted the guard. The police were called. I did not reach Ward 12 until 11.30pm.

My brother and sister-in-law were already at Mum's bedside. They sat on one side of her bed, and I on the other. Mum's breathing was loud at first. Taking turns, we spoke quietly, close to her 'good' ear.

Nurses Ann and Liz turned Mum, and her breathing eased, growing slighter and slighter. Who can tell what she took in, but we continued to talk quietly to her in turns. Everything became still and peaceful, in her, in us, in the ward.

At the end, I hardly realised what had happened; yet suddenly everything was different. We sat beside Mum for a little while longer. We had a talk with Nurse Ann. A doctor came to certify the death. We kissed Mum goodbye. By 2.30 am we were back at number 10 and went to bed. I blessed God for His goodness to me in Mum and Dad, and repeated, as I went to sleep,

'Parting is such sweet sorrow.'

Judy arrived from London. She and I visited Ward 12 to collect the doctor's statement of the cause of death and Mum's belongings, and to bid the nurses farewell with flowers.

One of the nurses took us over to the little chapel where Mum's body was resting. For a long time Judy stood at the foot of the bed, as if in conversation with Mum. I kept out of Judy's line of sight, at the back of the room. Later, Judy told me, 'She was there, waiting for me... There was a lot to say.'

The funeral took place six days later.

The flowers were purple and white, as Mum had wished. Many of the nurses and helpers in Ward 12 were present.

On the coffin, at the last moment, I laid a small bunch of lily of the valley from the back garden of number 10. They had flowered and spread there steadily over the forty-eight years since Dad had bought the house. Mum and Dad both loved them. On a card I wrote, 'To our much loved and much loving Father.'

It brought the two of them back together at the end, and for ever.

39
A Walk

FOUR YEARS LATER, on 1st August 2002, my brother and his wife, Judy and I are setting off on a special walk. We are on holiday together at Ringmore, a village about a mile from the sea at Challaborough.

With haversacks, cameras, binoculars and map, we walk past All Hallows church, with its square, grey tower and a small black spire perched on top of it, and then make our way along the narrow lanes to the small village of Kingston. We buy stamps in the Methodist church, which functions as a post office on two mornings a week, and then have lunch in the garden at the Dolphin Inn.

Meeting not a soul, we take the National Trust footpath and then join the coastal path at Fernycombe Point. From there we can see the waters of the estuary of the River Erme (so treacherous to swimmers) and the yellow, empty sands of the private beach at Mothecombe.

We climb the cliff path to Hoist Point, over three hundred feet above the sea, and we see the tors of Dartmoor, twenty miles to the north. To the south, twenty-six miles out at sea, is the Eddystone lighthouse, standing out sharply and clearly, well within the horizon granted us by the height of the cliffs and the clear air.

We are enjoying the secret, perfect weather of south Devon, the freshness and sunshine afforded by a low-pressure system, while the rest of the country suffers floods. It was often like this at the caravan at Challaborough in the 1950s and 1960s.

The smell of the sea, the warmth of the air and the fragrance of the grass on the cliffs cast a spell on us. The close-cropped turf puts a spring in our step and lifts our hearts.

As we walk, with the fields on our left hand and the sea on our right, my brother points out the buzzards high above us, mewing as they teach their young how to hunt; swallows and swifts, screaming in flight as they catch insects. The swifts are staying on rather later than usual this year. In a few spots we see cirl buntings, unique to this coast.

In the hedges there are banks of wild flowers: great mullein, purple toadflax, pink-purple toadflax, yellow toadflax, mugwort, hedge woundwort, enchanter's nightshade, pink perslane, hedge bedstraw, tufted vetch, fleabane, pineapple mayweed, fumitory, corn marigold; as well as the more common flowers, herb Robert, red campion, honeysuckle, scarlet pimpernel, speedwell, hawkbit and common cleavers.

At one stage, near the copse at Broad Cliff where Freshwater Brook plunges about a hundred feet straight down to the beach, a new path turns a little inland and tacks back and forth, in order to make the sheer slopes easier for walkers.

My brother recalls how, forty years ago, almost to the day, he walked this coast when the path still kept close to the cliff edge. On this section there had been steps, cut into the hillside. Dad was with him on that strenuous climb.

The two of them did the whole of the walk together, making a long hike from Challaborough via Ringmore, Kingston, Blackaport Cross, the path on the eastern bank of the Erme and then the cliffs, and back to the caravan. It amounts to fifteen miles in all, walked with only a drink of water from a tap in a farmyard as they made their way back to the caravan for tea with Mum.

Today the weather is perfect, but we meet no one else walking on the cliff path. Yet I sense the two of them, Dad and Mum together, in step with us on this walk, and along with them the One Whom they faithfully served so long, our Lord Jesus Christ, on Whom everything depends.

Epilogue

I owe the reader an answer to my own question, posed in the preface. My answer is this. It begins and ends with Jesus.

In the years that He walked this earth before His crucifixion and resurrection, Jesus was recognised by those who knew Him as more than an individual person, however gifted and dedicated. Those who knew Him best acknowledged Him as the supreme representative of Israel, God's chosen people, and of all mankind.

This humble person spoke of Himself as 'Son of Man', the One in Whom God's will was and would be accomplished, through self-sacrifice and death and then glorious triumph, so incorporating in Himself all those who accepted that they were part of Him. Jesus spoke of God as His Father, addressing Him in prayer in an intimate way. He was crucified and rose from the dead.

He lives for all eternity, with those who love Him as His limbs or branches, to share His glory as children of the Father, again for all eternity. Because Jesus lives, death cannot appal us. We belong to Jesus, now and forever.

As my beloved parents each said to me urgently in the months before their deaths, 'Everything depends on our Lord Jesus Christ. Everything depends on Jesus.'

It was this faith that inspired and sustained my parents. Nothing else could have done it, transforming their suffering into joy in the way that it did. God was with us. Much more can be said of this faith, but not here.

May I recommend three books to any reader wishing to go further? The first two are *Mere Christianity* by C.S. Lewis, written during the Second World War, and the same author's *Miracles*. They have never been bettered as an introduction to the faith. The third book, about the person of Jesus Christ, is *Encounters with Jesus* by Stuart Blanch. This is often out of print but is easily found as a second-hand book. It helps us approach in a scholarly and yet personal way the mystery of Jesus on whom everything depends.

Acknowledgements

Lines from 'The White Cliffs of Dover', by Alice Duer Miller, published by Methuen, 1941, are reproduced by permission of Pollinger Limited and the Estate of Alice Duer Miller.

An excerpt from *A Shaft of Sunlight* by Philip Mason, published by Andre Deutsch, 1979, is reproduced by permission of Mr Mason's family.

An excerpt from *George* by Emlyn Williams, published by Hamish Hamilton, 1961, is reproduced by permission of Mr Williams' literary executors, c/o the Maggie Nash Literary Agency.